EDMUND

THE UNTOLD STORY OF THE MARTYR-KING AND HIS KINGDOM

UPDATED EDITION - FULLY REVISED AND EXPANDED

MARK TAYLOR

EDMUND
The Untold Story of the Martyr-King and His Kingdom

For Mum and Dad

CONTENTS

ACKNOWLEDGEMENTS

All photography © Mark Taylor, with the following exceptions:

- St Edmund memorial coin photograph © Charles Muglestone

All illustrations © Mark Taylor, with the following exceptions:

- Plan of Sutton Hoo, modified from original maps by Carver and Green

- Map of the Lark – Gipping corridor, with data taken from Dymond and Martin

- Fornham Cursus, where Pennick and Devereux's map was used as reference

- Plan of Bury, modified from original maps by Dymond and Northeast et al

- Hundreds map, modified from maps originally utilised by Birch and Scarfe

- Kingdom of East Anglia, where maps by Hippisley Cox, Newton and Green were used as reference

- The Great Ditches, where maps by Hippisley Cox, Pennick and Devereux were used as reference

Thanks to the Rt Revd Charles Mugleston for use of the Psalm of St Edmund and the Edmund memorial coin images

Thanks to the staff at the Suffolk Records Office for their help

Thanks to Thornham Parva PCC and parish church staff

Thanks to the following authors, whose works have inspired this book: Nigel Pennick, David Dymond, Paul Devereux, Martin Carver, Brian Bates, Sam Newton, Bob Trubshaw

INTRODUCTION

On November 20th 869 Edmund, probably the last in a line of native East Anglian kings, was killed by invading Danes. According to legend Edmund was tied to a tree and scourged, shot with arrows and speared with javelins until he was covered with missiles 'like the bristles of a hedgehog.' He was then decapitated, his head thrown into a bramble bush and his body left where it lay. Later, both body and head were recovered. When placed together, they miraculously became whole again. The remains were stowed in a small wooden church close to the place of Edmund's death.

Numerous supernatural events were attributed to Edmund's body which, according to those who witnessed it, was immune to decay. Within twenty years of his death King Alfred declared him patron saint of England. His cult, at first a grass-roots movement, grew to dizzy heights once the body was moved to the monastery at Bury St Edmunds. Edmund's shrine became a focal point for wondrous happenings, particularly in relation to miracles of fertility and protection (his acts of revenge from beyond the grave on those who threatened the people of East Anglia are extraordinary.) Edmund's cult also rapidly gained popularity amongst the very Vikings who slaughtered him. 2,000 coins were minted in his memory bearing the inscription 'sce eadmund rex' (O St Edmund the King!) and were circulated within the area of the Danelaw. An indication of where Vikings settled lies in the naming of the parish church; it would often be dedicated to St Edmund. His cult spread as far north as Scandinavia and Iceland.

Edmund's shrine was all gold and marble, adorned with relics from other saints, and perpetually lit by four candles. It was one of England's most sacred sites, and certainly its most popular pilgrimage destination for a time. Royalty venerated the saint and attended his shrine on a number of occasions and, in turn, bequeathed land and indulgences to the abbey. At its peak, it was one of the most powerful monastic houses in Britain. A centre of artistic splendour and culture, the abbey entertained kings, housed parliaments and acquired an impressive library.

Churchgate Street - the Great Axis - looking towards the Norman Tower, Bury St Edmunds.

The Church was somewhat wary of the cult of saint-kings however. Edmund's martyrdom was not officially recognized until 250 years after his death. There were good reasons for caution, as Anglo-Saxon kings were channels for magical forces that guaranteed prosperity and good fortune for the people. Edmund was, in many ways, the ultimate example of this mysterious bond between god, king and land.

This book attempts to unravel that bond, which had its origins in early myth and religious practice. The interplay of Celtic, Anglo-Saxon and Viking cultures maintained and embroidered certain core ideas about sacred kingship, and this influenced the way in which Edmund's death was interpreted. The ebb and flow of belief, and the rich interweaving of Christian and pagan traditions, also shaped Edmund's early cult and his later sainthood; political and social concerns similarly affected the evolution of his myth. These common ideas explain his sudden popularity in death and his acceptance by both Anglo-Saxon and Viking, pagan and Christian. They define Edmund's relationship to the town of Bury St Edmunds and the surrounding countryside, and shed light on Edmund's status as a provider of fertility and protection.

Modern perceptions of Edmund are somewhat different to those earlier notions. Walking around Bury St Edmunds today, you would be forgiven for thinking Edmund was a fragile figure, a victim. In the middle of a roundabout, a sculpture shows him bound and riddled with arrows. Dame Elizabeth Frink's statue, next to St Edmundsbury cathedral, depicts a naked, vulnerable boy-king. And elsewhere, in Bernard Cornwell's

'King Alfred' series of novels, Edmund is nothing more than a holy fool. But the reality is he was a warrior-king, trading blows with the invading Danes to defend his lands, beloved by his people and ultimately prepared to sacrifice himself for them, and for the kingdom.

Edmund's Wolf - one of a number of sculptures related to Edmund located throughout Bury.

Edmund is now largely forgotten, a neglected martyr whose star began to wane when Edward III selected St George as a new elite and aristocratic patron saint in the 14th century. A number of recent worthy campaigns have attempted to reverse this decision and reinstate Edmund as the nation's patron saint. Bury's coat of arms – a crown and two crossed arrows – commemorate him, and this symbol can be found across the region. His name is used to adorn local ales and road names, but there is little awareness of Edmund's life and accomplishments. The location of his shrine is all but unmarked, overlooking tennis courts and in the stern shadow of the town's sugar beet factory. There is virtually nothing left of the abbey today, beyond a low maze of flint walls.

This book provides a new interpretation of Edmund's story. Others have spent considerable effort attempting to separate fact from fiction in his legend but, in all likelihood, these matters will never be resolved. Very little is known about him; only a handful of documents, place-names, coin finds and depictions reveal anything about this enigmatic martyr-king. Instead, this book focusses on his myth – the cultural weave that grew up around his martyrdom. Myths, after all, are created to address the specific needs of the time. By looking at the Edmund myth, and by interpreting its symbols, we may understand the era's diverse mix of identities, beliefs and preoccupations. This process will, in turn, help confirm Edmund's true significance and status as a divine sentinel-king in the tradition of other national heroes.

Although impossible to be certain, it is assumed that Edmund – which means 'wealth' and 'protection' – was born in approximately 841, son of Æthelweard or Ealhhere, brother-in-law to Æthelstan the king of Kent and, for a time, king of East Anglia. His mother was Edith.

As mentioned, very little is known about Edmund. Much of the information available comes from Dunstan, Abbot of Glastonbury. He heard the details of Edmund's martyrdom from the saint's ageing armour-bearer, whilst attending the court of the then King Æthelstan. He related the story to Abbo of Fleury, a French Benedictine monk, who recorded the details for posterity in a Latin passion some hundred years after Edmund's death. Royal saints were numerous in Anglo-Saxon England, but Edmund's death is perhaps unique amongst English martyrs; unlike Oswald, who was killed in battle, and Sigeberht, who refused to pick up a sword, Edmund was a warrior-king who *willingly* sacrificed himself in order to save his people.

He was probably the last native East Anglian king, ending a line that began with Wehha, legendary founder of the Wuffinga Anglo-Saxon royal dynasty. Some tales tell of Edmund's brother, Edwald, who was offered the crown but refused it, preferring instead a hermit's life at Cerne Abbas in Dorset. Two puppet kings, Æthelred and Oswald, are recorded as succeeding Edmund, but despite a coin discovery that hints at some continuity of East Anglian royalty, it is more probable that Æthelred and Oswald were either royalty installed from elsewhere by the Danes, or local East Anglian officials not of royal descent.

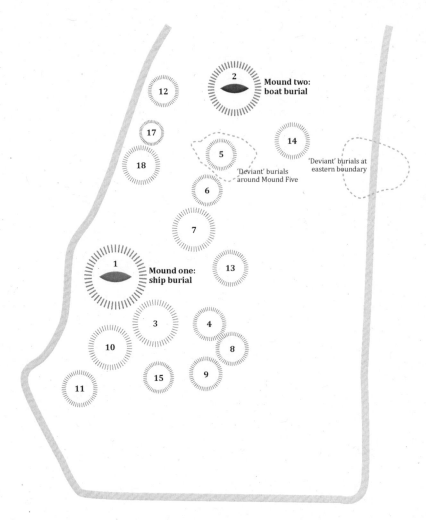

Plan of the Sutton Hoo burial site. The Wuffinga king Rædwald's burial was probably located at Mound One.

In 449 Angle, Saxon and Jutish warriors were, according to British cleric Gildas, invited into Britain to help defend the population against raids from Picts, Irish and continental warbands. Following Roman collapse and withdrawal some thirty years earlier, Britain could no longer properly defend its borders, although research suggests that post-Roman society was less chaotic than previously imagined. Led by Hengist and Horsa, this band of Germanic mercenaries liked Britain so much they decided to stay. There is no archaeological evidence for an Anglo-Saxon invasion, so it is assumed these migrants settled relatively peacefully, establishing control over time and ultimately carving England into mini-kingdoms. Hengist and Horsa founded the royal house of Kent; Ælle and his sons the South Saxons; Sledd the East Saxons, Creoda the kingdom of Mercia and Wehha the East Angles (to name but a few.) By 597 the majority of Anglo-Saxon kingdoms were already in existence. With their love of stories and wordplay, of small communities surrounded by nature, of fate, reputation and loyalty, the Anglo-Saxons moulded the East Anglia and England we still recognize today. In Domesday Book, Suffolk's 500 parish names are spelled very much as they are now.

Although Edmund's descent from the Wuffinga dynasty cannot be absolutely confirmed, it is often assumed. Originally from Jutland, the Wuffingas, which means 'the kin of the wolf', settled around Suffolk Sandlings, echoing earlier Neolithic and Bronze Age patterns. They were ultimately responsible for establishing the Kingdom of East Anglia, in the first quarter of the sixth century, by uniting an older group of settlers in the north – the North Folk – with their own South Folk. A royal power-base was later established in the south of the region at Rendlesham. Under them, the east of England thrived. It has been estimated that the population of East Anglia in the first half of the sixth century was 55,000 – one thirteenth of the total population of Britain.

The magnificent ship burial at the famous Sutton Hoo site near modern Woodbridge speaks of the region's wealth and influence. Situated on a promontory high above the River Deben, the cemetery, a major centre for high status burials, consists of twenty mounds. The largest – mound one – contained the ship burial, within which a Wuffinga king was likely interred, along with a stupendous array of grave goods. The helmet discovered amongst these items, and now so well known, has become a universal icon for the so-called Dark Ages. Along with the helmet, other finds included a mail coat, sword, shield, spears, a cauldron, gold and silver bowls, drinking horns, bottles, a standard and scepter, clothing and even a pillow. The most venerable Wuffinga king was Rædwald, who was acknowledged as overlord, or 'Bretwalda', by other English kings. At one point it was suggested that the body interred in mound one was the last pagan Wuffinga king, Æthelhere, who died in 654. Since then, the consensus has shifted to Rædwald, the Bretwalda himself. This certainly explains the high-status nature of the burial.

Although there is no evidence for an Anglo-Saxon invasion, some recent DNA studies have shown that an overwhelming proportion of males in central England carry an Anglo-Saxon genetic signature. This is in contrast to Wales, Scotland, northern and southwest England, where DNA profiles suggest different origins. Whether this genetic dominance is a result of Anglo-Saxon mass migration or some other event is not clear; the lack of documentary or archaeological evidence for invasion suggests that, instead, a relatively small Anglo-Saxon influx, probably a ruling elite, was able to perpetuate its genetic signature in five generations. Perhaps Gildas was close to the truth when he described Hengist and Horsa's band of mercenaries arriving in only three longboats. It is highly likely that Anglo-Saxons and Britons intermingled, but the extent is unclear. British expulsion or apartheid would certainly have accelerated the spread of Anglo-

Saxon DNA, but it is equally plausible that male immigrants took Romano-Celtic wives, and the indigenous population gradually switched from Roman to Anglo-Saxon cultural identities. Celts probably continued to live in East Anglia, at least until the 6th century. And although the move to Anglo-Saxon society was ultimately comprehensive, Celtic, Anglo-Saxon and Norse cultures continued to interact, trade and influence one another. Edmund's own story, in relation to traditions of sacred kingship, bear this out; his myth reveals continuity of tradition stretching back to at least the Iron Age.

Small pockets of Celtic peoples may have lived in the region into the Middle and Late Saxon periods, but those who rejected Anglo-Saxon society likely relocated to western Britain or were placed under migrant control. The few who did remain perhaps survived in the Fens as serfs or outlaws until the 10th century, raiding churches and communities around Huntington. The 2006 Channel 4 documentary 'Face of Britain' revealed that modern East Anglians are overwhelmingly Anglo-Saxon in their genetic composition; in fact, they provide the closest match in the whole of Britain. As well as dialect and names, the folk of modern East Anglia even share facial similarities with the original Germanic migrants: a heavy brow, high cheekbones, a smaller jaw and a split nose and chin. This facial matching was carried out in Bury St Edmunds, where plenty of 'Anglo Saxon' DNA appeared to be on display. The lack of Celtic place names still in use reinforces this switch; perhaps just fifteen names with a Celtic origin remain in Suffolk, including Walpole, Clare, Walton and Dunwich.

The Great Heathen Army

Writers after Abbo have attempted to deny Edmund's East Anglian credentials, claiming he was born in Nuremberg of Old Saxon parentage; in this version of events, his parents were Alcmund and Siwara. But Abbo's *Passio* certainly did promote a dynastic link with the Wuffinga line through the use of a wolf motif; the wolf found protecting Edmund's severed head can be seen as a kind of guardian spirit of the East Anglian dynasty, establishing Edmund's affinity with the Wuffinga 'wolf-kin'. The most credible theory for Edmund's parentage suggests Ealhhere, brother-in-law to King Æthelstan of Kent, as Edmund's father. This would make Edith (Æthelstan's sister) Edmund's mother. On Egbert's death, Æthelwulf installed his son Æthelstan as king of East Anglia, Sussex, Kent and Surrey. It is assumed that Ealhhere was an East Anglian noble before he married into the Wessex dynasty. Æthelstan, a childless king, supposedly near-adopted the young Edmund and bequeathed him the throne of East Anglia.

Later writers also expounded on Edmund's early life. He was, for instance, marked for greatness before he was born, being the subject of prophesy: a Roman woman declared to his father that from him would come a son whose fame, like the sun, would illuminate the four quarters of the world and bring many to Christ. King Offa of Mercia, on pilgrimage to Jerusalem, passed through Saxony and visited his cousin Alcmund. By this time Edmund was a boy of twelve years. Offa was so struck by the boy's physical and spiritual beauty that he handed Edmund his coronation ring, effectively inviting him to become his adopted son and heir. Edmund agreed. Offa removed the ring and continued on to the Holy Lands, but fell ill and died, although not before dispatching his nobles to Saxony. They bore Offa's coronation ring and a command to entrust the kingdom of East Anglia to Edmund's rule. At fourteen years old, Edmund sailed for Hunstanton to realize his destiny. On arrival he disembarked in a dry riverbed and kissed the ground. In response, twelve healing springs gushed forth from the earth. These days, there is little if no support for this version of Edmund's origins.

Edmund was crowned in 855 by Humbert, Bishop of Elmham, possibly on a sacred hill at Attleborough, Bulmer or St Bures, or at St Gregory's church in Sudbury. Abbo describes Edmund as a model king who ruled for over a decade; his fitness to rule, eloquence, manly beauty and quiet devotion were coupled with his eschewing of all vain arrogance; his character coupled the cunning of serpents with the harmlessness of doves. He took generous care of his kingdom and people. He embodied the right balance of the Good and the Beautiful, the combination of virtues that could create the perfect nobleman. Edmund was, in every sense, an ideal ruler.

Yet his rule was blighted by the incursions of the Viking 'Great Heathen Army' into East Anglia. The first Viking raid on English soil occurred in 789. Four years later, the infamous raid on Lindisfarne took place, where, according to Alcuin, the Danes 'miserably destroyed God's church… by rapine and slaughter.' Apart from a few scattered raids on other Northumbrian monasteries, little more was heard of the Vikings until 835, when they began to attack southern England. By the mid ninth century, raids were commonplace across northern Europe. Writing in the 860s, Ermantarius, a monk from the island of Noirmoutier on the west coast of France recorded how:

The number of ships increases, the endless flood of Vikings never ceases to grow bigger. Everywhere Christ's people are the victims of massacre, burning and plunder. The Vikings over-run all that lies before them, and none can withstand them.

In 865, the arrival of the Heathen Army substantially ratcheted up the Viking threat. Consisting of up to 2,000 troops, it was nominally led by Ivarr the Boneless, but in reality was a loose amalgamation of various warbands. One or more of these was commanded by three brothers: Hinguar, Healfdene and Hubba, bent on revenge for the death of their father, Ragnar Lodbrog. Depending on the source material, Lodbrog was murdered either at the hands of King Edmund's wayward huntsman, Bern, or the English King Alle of Northumbria. Apocryphal stories from this period attest to Edmund's prowess and courage, defeating the enemy in many encounters. Yet after a period of conflict Edmund chose to appease the invaders with a gift of horses, which was accepted.

After Edmund had successfully sued for peace, the Danes were unable to prosecute their war and so left Edmund's kingdom for a time, marching north to Eoferwic (York) and ravaging territories in Yorkshire and Northumberland. At the end of the year the Heathen Army swept into Mercia and took Nottingham; King Æthelred and his son Alfred converged on the city to offer their support.

The Danes swept back towards East Anglia; Hubba concentrated on raiding the Fenland monasteries at Ely and Peterborough, while Hinguar proceeded to Newmarket Heath. There he met resistance at a set of earthworks known as Devil's Dyke (or at the time 'Holy

Edmund's Fortifications'), led by one of Edmund's earls, but the Saxon defenders were virtually wiped out. The Danes then proceeded to Thetford and took winter quarters there. Hinguar sent a messenger to Edmund with terms for his surrender, namely that Edmund give up his kingdom and wealth, renounce his faith and acknowledge Hinguar as his master.

Edmund consulted with his bishop, declaring 'I would rather die fighting so that my people might continue to possess their native land.' The bishop advised Edmund to either flee or submit, but the king asserted that 'it was never my way to flee. I would rather die for my country if I need to.'

Edmund rejected Hinguar's offer outright, unless the Dane converted to Christianity (we can assume Hinguar refused) and, with what remained of his forces, marched on Thetford. A bitter seven-hour battle raged and the Anglo-Saxons were defeated. The king withdrew, his army decimated. Edmund learned that Hubba's men were advancing to bolster the depleted Danish lines. He was no doubt sick at heart, knowing that, despite his many victories, the war was lost; the majority of his men were dead, and Danish savagery would never cease until they had conquered East Anglia. At this point, one senses, Edmund knew that in order to save his people he would need to surrender. But, having rejected the Danish terms, surrender was no longer an option; nothing less than his death would be acceptable; he would need to sacrifice himself for the sake of his kingdom.

A depiction of Edmund, hiding beneath Goldbrook Bridge, Hoxne.

At that time, Edmund was staying at a location known as Hægelisdun. The Danes sent men after him and he was captured, either in his hall, or under a bridge, or in a church. In later folk tales Edmund was dragged from a castle by the Danes, but pretended he was one of the king's followers, not the king himself. He hid under a bridge but the glint from his golden spurs was spotted by a newly-wed couple, who betrayed him. In response Edmund cursed all bridal couples who might cross the bridge in future, and until relatively recently wedding parties would avoid it.

Slaughter At Hægelisdun

Either way, on 20th November 869, at the age of twenty-nine years, Edmund was brought before the Danish leaders and, possibly in front of his own captured men, tortured. He was tied to a tree and scourged, shot with arrows and speared with javelins until he was covered with missiles 'like the bristles of a hedgehog.' Finally, he was beheaded. John Lydgate's 15th century *vita* describes how Edmund's holy cousin, St Fremund, avenged the king's death, but was himself killed while praying and thanking God for the victory over the Danish invaders.

The Danes eventually departed for Reading, discarding Edmund's head in thick brambles. One of Edmund's men, possibly his armour-bearer, had observed his king's death. He and others began the process of searching for the body and decapitated head. They found the former, but the latter caused them to track deep into the woods. They called out 'where are you now friend?' In response a voice cried 'here, here, here.' They rushed to the source and found Edmund's head, still capable of speech, clasped between the paws of a great wolf, who protected it from the other forest animals. They took the head and the guardian-wolf followed them until both parts of the corpse were safe, then it loped back into the woods. The head then became miraculously reunited with the body, according to folklore.

It is traditionally thought that Edmund died at Hoxne in Suffolk, close to the River Waveney, or Hellesdon near Norwich. But perhaps the best fit for the location of Hægelisdun is Bradfield St Clare, where a nearby field is called 'Hellesdon Ley', and a moated house called 'Sutton Hall' lies a mile to the south. Both sites are roughly five miles from Bury. An OS map of 1904 shows a nearby wood – possibly ancient woodland originally part of the Sutton Hall estate – named as King's Grove; the name is still in use today. Yet an earlier tithe map of 1844 apportions it only as The Grove. Although the Bradfield St Clare / Hægelisdun theory is relatively new (1985), a landowner saw fit to change the name at some point between 1844 and 1903; the reason may have nothing to do with St Edmund whatsoever, yet it is tempting to speculate that this could be the woodland where Edmund's head was found.

The Bradfield St Clare location is given further credence when considered in relation to the Lark-Gipping corridor. These two rivers formed a navigable route from the northwest to the southeast of East Anglia, and constituted an important cultural and political boundary, likely demarcating the southern edge of the kingdom. Archaeological evidence shows that both rivers were settled from the early Anglo-Saxon era, supporting the theory that this was a significant thoroughfare. Danish raiders could reasonably have used this waterway to traverse the region, entering from either The Wash in the north or the Orwell in the south. The pattern of Viking church burning and raiding at Bury, Soham and Ely also corresponds with the route of this corridor. More significantly, Bradfield St Clare lies close by, immediately endowing the location with strategic significance. It is possible then to construct a scenario whereby Edmund, defeated at Thetford, retreated south, perhaps passing through Bury – ironically, the later location of his shrine – to Hægelisdun at Bradfield St Clare. Whether his ultimate destination lay further south in Essex, or to the east at Rendlesham, we cannot know. But it is possible that Hubbar, fresh from raiding Fenland monasteries, then sailed east along the Lark-Gipping corridor to intercept Edmund while Hinguar's men advanced from the north. Probably because of Viking activity in the region, Edmund's corpse was not immediately transferred to Bury. Initially his body was buried close to where he was killed, at a place called Sutton (the 'Sutton Hall' near Bradfield St Clare), beneath a simple chapel. Legend tells of an early miracle occurring here: one night, a blind man and his son became lost while walking through the woods nearby. They found Edmund's chapel and decided to spend the night inside. A brilliant light was conjured and, thinking a fire had broken out, they began to panic. The light faded, the chapel was intact and they returned to sleep. At dawn, the man awoke to discover his blindness had been cured. It was recorded later that 'miracles happened frequently at his grave.'

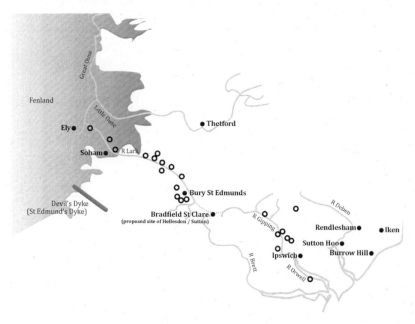

Map showing the Lark-Gipping corridor, and the pattern of Anglo-Saxon settlement and Viking church raiding in the region.

In 903 the transfer of Edmund was completed, accompanied by the Bishop of Elmham and major East Anglian clergy. Upon disinterring the body, a further miracle was revealed:

[Edmund] was entirely fresh as if he were alive, with an uncorrupted body, and his neck, which had been cut through, was healed. There was as it were a silken thread about his red neck, as an indication to the world how he was slain. Also the wounds which the heathens had inflicted on his body with their frequent shots, were healed through the grace of the heavenly God.

Edmund's body was not only uncorrupted, but showed signs of vitality: nails and hair continued to grow, and were regularly cut once a year by 'venerable women', one of whom was named Oswen. The corpse was placed in a relatively plain timber round church within the grounds of the monastery.

In 925 Beodericsworth changed its name to St Edmundsbury, but fresh Viking raids began. Edmund's body was moved to the safety of London, lest the Vikings attempted to destroy the figurehead of a cult representing East Saxon resistance. In the care of a monk named Ethelwine or Egelwin, numerous miracles occurred en route: healings, miraculous river crossings and divine retribution against a careless priest. In 1013 the body was returned, with further miracles accompanying the journey back to Bury.

Sweyn Forkbeard was king of the Danes and, following his successful invasion, king of England also. He visited Bury in 1014, demanding tax from the lands of the abbey, and threatening to burn the town. The townsfolk refused the pay up, instead beseeching St Edmund to protect them. A monk who daily attended to the saint's corpse, by the name of Ailwin, had a vision in which St Edmund complained about the treatment of his people. Ailwin communicated this message to Sweyn, who in turn delivered an insolent reply. The next day, amidst his soldiers, Sweyn was stabbed with Edmund's own dagger. Shortly thereafter, the Danish king was dead.

Cnut, son of Sweyn, was a major benefactor to the religious house. On St Luke's Day 1032, when Edmund's shrine was consecrated, Cnut offered the saint a votive gold crown from his own head. Edward the Confessor shared a similar devotion. Royal interest in the saint went beyond the norm, with Edward usually walking the last mile to Edmund's shrine on foot. This veneration can be attributed to a number of factors. Firstly, Edmund was by this time patron saint of all England, and he therefore warranted a certain level of respect. He was the personification of Christian virtue: righteous, brave, meek and truthful. And as we shall see shortly, he also embodied an ancient tradition of sacrificed god-kings who bestowed good health to his land and subjects. Because of his significance, Edmund rapidly gained status as a protector of the people of East Anglia, the 'glory and shield of the East Angles' in the face of further upheavals.

Three miracles occurred at the Bury shrine to further cement Edmund's reputation: firstly he struck immobile a group of eight thieves who attempted to break into his church and steal the sacred (and valuable) objects within. Edmund froze the thieves where they stood, outside the church, until morning. They were brought before Bishop Theodred, who condemned them to death at the gallows, although he regretted not showing them mercy 'always until the end of his life.'

On another occasion, a rich noble visited St Edmund's shrine 'with exceeding arrogance and insolently ordered that the holy saint be shown to him so that he might see whether Edmund was whole.' On seeing the body, the noble was inflicted with madness, his life ending 'wretchedly in an evil death.'

Further evidence of Edmund's ability to mete out supernatural retribution is provided in the tale of Leofstan, a monk who dared open the saint's coffin to examine the body. In the process, his hands were paralysed and could not be cured. Edward I sent his own physician – Baldwin – to attend to the monk, but to no avail. Leofstan died in 1065 and was buried at the foot of St Edmund's shrine. Baldwin, a friend of both Edward and William of Normandy, was selected as abbot of Bury and remained there following the Norman Conquest.

In John Lydgate's retelling, Edmund's miracles consist of two visions, two episodes of rescue, three violent instances of revenge and another three acts of punishment followed by forgiveness, as well as some minor healings. Edmund mostly embodies the distinctive features of a knight rather than those of a saint. In another document there are 55 reported miracles: 27 are related to healing, nine to revenge, seven to visions, six to salvations and one to liberation. This roll call clearly emphasizes Edmund's healing power.

Body Of A Martyr

Following Abbot Baldwin's expansion of the abbey church, Edmund's body was brought from Cnut's round church to his new shrine at the church's east end. Jocelyn of Brakelond recorded a fire breaking out in the abbey church in 1198, which saw St Edmund's shrine suffer some damage amid rumours that his head had been burnt. Samson decided to check the body himself, so the coffin, standing on a tray of wood, was uncovered:

Affixed to the outside, over the breast of the martyr, lay an angel of gold, about the length of a man's foot, holding in one hand a golden sword and in the other a banner. Underneath it, there was a hole in the lid of the coffin, where the ancient custodians of the martyr had been wont to lay their hands, for the purpose of touching the sacred body. And over the figure of the angel was this verse inscribed 'Martiris ecce zoma servat Michaelis agalma [This is the Martyr's garment, which Michael's image guards].'

The coffin was removed and carried to a nearby table. Sixteen nails around the lid were unfastened, revealing the body of Edmund the martyr within. The head was united to the body, resting on a pillow, and the whole was wrapped in veils of linen and silk. Samson observed 'the feet standing stiff up, like the feet of a man who had died that day.' All in all the body was unharmed, but still Samson deposed the keepers of the shrine, and 'appointing new ones, and establishing rules, so that the holy places should be more carefully and diligently kept.'

During the Reformation, the great abbey was dissolved and the relics lost, or destroyed.

The location of St Edmund's body is also unknown. The abbey's monks initially transferred the remains to a secret place for safekeeping, along with the solid gold angel affixed to his coffin. At some point they seem to have been transferred to France, then back to England, and kept in a private chapel at Arundel Castle in West Sussex. It has also been suggested that Edmund's body is buried beneath tennis courts close to the ruins of Bury abbey.

It is difficult to discern the ultimate source of the content of Edmund's *vita*. Did it originate with Abbo, or Dustan, or Edmund's armour-bearer, or even folk-tales that were already currency at this time? Asser's Life of Alfred does not mention Edmund's martyrdom, simply that he was killed by the Danes. Yet Abbo's *Passio* is accepted as the authoritative source for an understanding of Edmund's life and death. If Abbo did take liberties, perhaps they were modest. For instance, it is likely the monk seized an opportunity to establish Edmund's royal credentials and kingly qualities, and to highlight non-violence as the proper path of a holy king. But what are we to make of the more fantastical elements of Edmund's story: the wolf, the severed head rejoining the body, the many miracles? Are they to be treated as commonplace saintly qualities to exaggerate Edmund's holiness? Or as symbols, pointing to hidden meanings? Or are they accounts of real events?

Some claim Abbo's Passio is no more than a patchwork of borrowings from other lives of the saints, that Abbo adapted these standard motifs as he saw fit. But writing over 100 years after the event, Abbo was effectively recounting a myth-making process. It is reasonable to assume that Edmund's story began with his followers, with the people who witnessed his death and endured the aftermath of Viking subjugation. This book proposes that a myth was purposefully crafted around Edmund, based on his outstanding qualities in life, that related him to an ancient tradition of sacred kingship. The purpose of this was to threefold: firstly, it conferred on Edmund an authority in death; he retained a binding power over society and the land that the Danes could not break; if anything, his murder strengthened it. This gave comfort and inspiration to Edmund's loyal followers: the Danes may have become nominal rulers in East Anglia but, through his sacrifice, Edmund remained the true king. Secondly, it endowed Edmund with supernatural powers; the king became a conduit for divine inspiration, justice, fecundity and legitimate rule. Thirdly, these traditions of sacred kingship were common to both pagan and Christian, Celtic, Saxon and Norse cultures; by association with them, Edmund the martyr succeeded in uniting Saxon and Viking in veneration of him. This weave of influences laid the groundwork for Edmund's longevity and patron sainthood. And they ultimately revealed him as an archetypal hero-king; an East Anglian Arthur representing the noblest aspirations: order, moral rectitude and the welfare of the kingdom. Like Arthur, Edmund embodies a fundamental mythic truth: the land and the king are one.

THE SLAIN KING

Sce Eadmund Rex

Why did Edmund allow himself to be captured and killed? Why was he a willing victim? One might argue that it was a selfless (or selfish) act, to imitate Christ by offering himself, unarmed, as a sacrificial lamb. In so doing, it brought him closer to God whilst simultaneously guaranteeing his martyr status, and subsequent sainthood. Edmund was a deeply pious Christian, and he may well have been driven by this ultimate test of faith. At the very least, his chronicler Abbo was no doubt keen to illustrate Edmund's sanctity by drawing comparisons between Christ and the holy king. Abbo introduced the notion that death was Edmund's ultimate duty as a Christian regent.

In Abbo's *Passio*, Edmund's motivation for offering himself up appears to be the welfare of his people and kingdom. He claims 'I would rather die fighting so that my people might continue to possess their native land… I would rather die for my country if I need to.' But were there really any practical benefits to Edmund's sacrifice? He was a virgin king, with no heirs. His death, whatever might cause it, would create a void that other pretenders would rush to fill, inviting conflict and upheaval. Ultimately, his slaughter at the hands of Danish invaders yielded no positive outcome for his people. Their king had died – seemingly an unnecessary sacrifice; their fate was pagan rule, and subjugation to the Viking yoke. The powerful bond between king and *thegn* was broken, the loss of their king a devastating event. A retainer without a lord was essentially an outcast, with

Both faces of the coin minted between 895 and 905 in memory of Edmund.

no place in society. In the Anglo-Saxon poem 'The Wanderer', a loyal retainer describes the impact of his lord's death:

Then his wounds lie more heavy in his heart,
Aching for his lord. His sorrow is renewed;
The memory of kinsmen sweeps through his mind;
Joyfully he welcomes them, eagerly scans
His comrade warriors. Then they swim away again...
...I mourn the gleaming cup, the warrior in his corselet,
The glory of the prince. How that time has passed away,
Darkened under the shadow of night as if it had never been.

In the wake of Edmund's death, it would have seemed as though pagan might had triumphed over Christian virtue. But in Christian terms Edmund was not truly defeated; the decision to embrace death was a victory of the holy king's self-sacrifice. His martyrdom represented the true and final conquest of good over evil, and he became holy in both life and death.

Surprisingly, Edmund's cult rapidly gained popularity amongst East Anglia's Viking settlers. 2,000 coins were minted in memory of Edmund between 895 and 905 bearing the inscription 'sce eadmund rex' (O St Edmund the King!), and were circulated within the area of the Danelaw; it is likely that these coins were minted by the Danes themselves. Why should Edmund be venerated amongst the very group who killed him? It has been suggested that the Danes paid lip-service to Edmund's cult in order to control the local population or, conversely, that the Danes adopted the cult in order to ease their settlement into an otherwise hostile environment. Viking settlers in the region tended to retain their own identities; they were separated by cultural and religious boundaries and, for a time, were a people apart. It is not clear whether they fully integrated at all. Years of warfare, not to mention the Danish slaughter of Edmund, no doubt generated resentment towards them. Unlike the northern Danelaw, there is little evidence of their impact on place names in East Anglia.

Another hypothesis is that Anglo-Saxon and Danes alike were united in their veneration of Edmund because his death represented not just a significant Christian sacrifice, but an echo of earlier practices, the roots of which resided in a shared heritage and deep-seated ideas about sacred kingship. Edmund's was a highly symbolic death, and the mythic symbolism embedded in his story would have had resonance for all, whether pagan, Christian, Anglo-Saxon or Viking. Within Celtic, Anglo-Saxon and Norse society, kingship was a sacred office guarded by elaborate traditions. Anglo-Saxon culture, in particular, introduced new concepts of kingship. One such was the notion that the primary allegiance of an individual was no longer to a family, or a tribal deity, but to a real territory and its leader. This lord–retainer relationship was absolutely paramount; it defined the context in which kinship, moral values and heroic reputations were forged. Kings were esteemed so highly because they were descended from gods. They functioned as conduits for divine energy, a magical force that promised fertility and good luck for the kingdom. As well-springs of vitality, kings embodied the seasonal cycles of life, death and rebirth represented first by solar and corn deities, then by Woden, and finally Christ. In this way the health of the regent, in every sense, was paramount; he defined the mystical link between heaven and earth, god, king and the land. If the king was unfit to rule, the kingdom and the people suffered. These Anglo-Saxon concepts of kingship are rooted in the ancient pre-Christian tradition referred to here as the 'slain king.' The slain king wore a number of different guises, but remained a fundamental dogma of the early religions of Europe and beyond. In essence it proposed that the god and his qualities were embodied in a sacred king or priest. The wellbeing of the king or priest affected the wellbeing of his people. Thus, if the kingdom suffered through famine, plague or war, then the king's ability to rule – and the gods' favour – was called into question. One important facet of the slain king tradition is sacrifice. Kings were ritually slaughtered at the height of their powers to ensure the ongoing prosperity of the kingdom; often this sacrifice was entered into willingly by the regent, in recognition of his role as a conduit for divine energy. Ritual killing, human sacrifice and king-slaying were, if not widespread, certainly important components of Scandinavian society up to and after Edmund's reign.

The Slain God

The sacred king was himself a physical embodiment of the tradition of the slain *god*, a category of deity who dies and is reborn, reflecting the natural cycle of life, death and rebirth. In the earliest cultures, this cycle of death and rebirth was recognized and venerated as a fundamental component of earthly existence – from the dying of the sun at the end of the day and its rebirth the next morning, to the cycle of the seasons, themselves a function of the sun's weakness in midwinter and vigour in midsummer. The cycles and their constituent parts were personified, and their mysteries recounted in myths – foundation stories of gods and heroes. The slain gods of antiquity typically represented either the regenerative powers of the sun, or of vegetation (corn or barley being the archetypal grains in this association.) For example, the legends of Adonis, Osiris and Isis, Demeter and Persephone, Dionysus, Attis and Mithras all attest to the powerful, symbiotic connections believed to exist between the health of the gods, the welfare of the king, the success of the kingdom and the fecundity of the natural world. Behind all these myths lay the possibility of eternal life – the potential for immortality within the cycle of life, death and rebirth; the mystery of life-in-death.

Osiris, for instance, is perhaps the best illustration of the slain-god-and-king myth, in that he was both a beloved human king of Egypt, and a powerful deity. Osiris was murdered by Seth, god of darkness and chaos. He was lured into an ornate chest, which was bolted, sealed and thrown into the Nile. When Isis, his wife, found the chest Osiris was already dead, but she roused him to life temporarily so that he may impregnate her, ultimately giving birth to Horus – a god associated with the sky, sun and moon, and whose 'eye of Horus' became a talisman of protection. Seth, learning of Horus's birth, located the corpse of Osiris and, in his fury, cut it into sixteen pieces, scattering them across the land. The sun god Ra sent Anubis to help restore Osiris to permanent life, by the performing of certain rites. Osiris was then granted an eternal kingdom in the Land of Silence as Lord of the Underworld. Thus, Osiris was a good and much-loved king who suffered a violent death but was resurrected and thereafter worshipped as a deity. In him the Egyptians saw the promise of eternal life, so long as similar rites were performed

Edmund was tied to an oak tree, according to legend. The oak is full of symbolism in Celtic and Germanic traditions.

over their own dead bodies.

The slain king tradition's essential practice involved the ritual slaughter of the king-priest-god at the most propitious time, in order to ensure the fertility of the land. The king's own life force was so sympathetically bound up with the prosperity of the whole country that, at the first sign of his powers failing (or even before), the king was sacrificed. Ironically, this was an expression of the community's profound veneration for him, and its desire to preserve the regenerative spirit that flowed through their regent. In this respect the king was a willing victim; he understood the rules of kingship, and shared a desire to maintain the health of the land and the people. Death was not equated with annihilation, but rather participation in the cosmic cycle of death and rebirth. The blood and flesh of the sacrifice lived on, distributed amongst the community; parts of the body were buried in fields to ensure the harvest. Sacrifice also freed the king's inner spirit; heaven and earth were united as his vital energy renewed the kingdom. He was, in effect, a bridge between two worlds. Thus, the king is often depicted hanging from, or tied to, a tree.

The idea of trees as gateways between the worlds is not new. Seahenge is a relatively small circle of 55 wooden uprights, located on the border of land and sea on the north Norfolk coast. An oak tree at the centre of the circle may have been a mortuary table to hold the dead – an altar where carrion was picked clean before interment elsewhere. It could also have represented a liminal meeting point between the mortal realm and the underworld, a parallel upside-down universe. The tree was perhaps a gateway for transferring the spirits of the dead to the afterlife. In Norse myth the World Tree Yggdrassill spreads downwards and upwards, its roots and branches uniting several different worlds or realms. The tree is a ladder between worlds, traversed in shamanic activities to obtain knowledge and wisdom. His sacrifice occuring upon a tree, the slain king was at one with heaven and earth; he represented procreative power, the seed of life. Sacrifice of the king was eventually replaced by animal and then plant, the latter personified in the corn god. Later veneration of Osiris, for example, incorporated annual rites that coincided with the seasonal agricultural cycle and the swelling of the Nile. In spring, effigies of Osiris, seeded with corn, would sprout, illustrating his procreative powers; he was the seed of life; the crops literally grew through him. In sacrificing his body, scattering it across the land, he fertilized the earth and ensured his people a good harvest.

In Northern European tradition, there is ample evidence of the slain king in practice, including human sacrifice. While Irish Celtic culture may not be the original source of the slain king ritual, it is perhaps the best-known. In 2011 an Iron Age body was recovered from a bog in County Laois, Ireland. The National Museum of Ireland's Head of Antiquities, Ned Kelly, believed cuts on the body suggested a ritual killing:

Irish kings in the ancient period were replaced after a number of years. The old king would be sacrificed and a new king chosen. It ties in with their religious beliefs surrounding the solar deity (male) and the deity of the land (female). The king ties in with the solar cycle – the waxing and waning of the sun. The idea was that the king was married to the sovereignty, or the land. The goddess would become old and withered and she would need a new young consort to return her to youth and vigour and beauty. So the old king would be killed and a new one take his place. They wouldn't have been that old, either.

Amongst the high Kings of Ireland, it was recorded that, in the reign of virtuous King Conaire, the fish were plentiful in the rivers; there was an abundance of everything and fair weather prevailed. But under a bad monarch, such as King Cairbre, 'there was not one grain in the ear, one acorn on the oak, or one nut on the hazel.' Thus, a king's personal qualities were linked to the general wellbeing of the land.

In 1984 a peat body was found in Britain just outside Manchester, dating from 50AD. Known as Lindow Man, it has been suggested the body is that of a Celtic king, prince or Druid. His willing sacrifice showed evidence of a ritual 'triple death' to three Celtic deities: Taranis, Esus and Teutates, to ensure prosperity for the community and protection from their Roman enemies.

Anglo-Saxon society was undoubtedly aware of the ancient traditions of sacred kingship, not least because of contact with Celtic societies in either mainland Britain or Ireland. These principles of kingship were already present, to some extent, in Anglo-Saxon culture, but the best evidence of Celtic continuity lies in grave goods found in mound one at Sutton Hoo. Thought to be the burial-place of King Rædwald, the goods include an enigmatic sceptre and a shield and purse bearing bird motifs. One theory suggests that the sceptre, an emblem of the king's authority, expresses in its symbolism Celtic ideas of kingship: the king as a binding link between earth and sky, upper and lower worlds; as a source of inspirational law-giving speech, and an embodiment of the contract between the people and their tribal god. Through the binding injunctions of kingship described on the sceptre's designs, the king's right judgment ensured the beneficent action of the elements and, in turn, the flourishing of nature and community. The bird motifs on purse and shield support this cosmology.

Celtic ideas of sacred kingship could also have influenced Scandinavian practices. The Ynglinga Saga is a 12th century tale by Snorri Sturluson, retelling an earlier poem. An instance of ritual king-slaying can be found within, in the form of the 9th century Swedish King Dómaldi, who was cursed with bad luck by his stepmother and ritually killed to ensure a good harvest:

During his [Dómaldi's] reign, there was famine and starvation in Sweden... The chieftans held a meeting and agreed unanimously that Dómaldi, their king, was the cause of the famine, so they decided to attack and kill him for a good harvest. And that is what they did. They reddened the altars with his blood...

In another contemporary document, the king is described as being hung to the corn mother 'for the fertility of the crops.' The Ynglings dynasty traced their descent from Frey, goddess of fertility.

A further example is provided by Halfdan the Black, another Ynglings king, who died in 860 and was therefore contemporary with Edmund. It was related that the king had been such an excellent ruler that, on his death, various chieftans requested that they might bury the body in their province, as it would bring abundance to those who obtained it.

In an echo of the slain king tradition, Halfdan was cut up into four pieces and buried in different parts of the kingdom to ensure the fruitfulness of the earth. Similarly, Oswald of Northumbria's body, ritually dismembered by the pagan king Penda, was distributed between Lindisfarne, Bamburgh and Bardney.

The concept of a king's 'life force' living on after his death to fertilise the land would have been familiar to Celts, Britons, Anglo-Saxons and Danes alike. The Celts understood this force as *nwyvre*. The Anglo-Saxons perceived the existence of *haelu*, a generalized life force that conferred good health, luck and prosperity, and was the source of all vitality. It was generated in the head, and flowed through the spine to the rest of the body. Haelu was suffused throughout the cosmos, as much a part of trees, plants, the earth and animals as humans. Amongst the Vikings, the vital animating power of creation was *ond*; it was a chaotic energy, yet took shape as manifest reality. It was also believed that life force lingered after death, and could be transferred to others via the consumption of blood and brains. These, and the specific role of a king's life-giving energy, correspond to the ancient Egyptian notion of *ka* – a vital force flowing from god through the king, by which the king directed the forces of nature for the benefit of the community.

A similar, but subtly different Anglo-Saxon concept was *mana* or *heil*, a force distinct from physical power or strength, the possession of which guaranteed success and good fortune. It was an attribute of kings, and it infused not just an individual regent but also the entire genealogy. Its source was the dynasty's progenitor – typically Woden, but later Christ. In this context, the king's role was to maintain favour with the tribal god. In doing so, he would effectively channel good fortune into the entire community and become a charismatic embodiment of that magical force.

Woden's Son

After the first tranche of Viking incursions (during which Edmund was slaughtered), King Alfred re-organized his royal genealogy. Like the houses of Kent, Essex, the Wuffingas and others, the Wessex dynasty began with Woden. Christian conversion meant the genealogy needed modification and so, as documented in the Anglo-Saxon Chronicle for the year 855, the Wessex royal family tree was extended to incorporate a pre-Woden Christian lineage. It included such notable antecedents as Noah, Enoch, Seth, Adam and, ultimately, Christ – the dynasty's progenitor. Interestingly, three of the new names preceding Woden were *Beaw, Sceldwa* and *Sceaf* (depending on the source and translation.) Various meanings have been attributed to these names, which translate as 'Barley', 'Shield' and 'Sheaf'. Barley is the son of Shield, and both are descendents of Sheaf. One interpretation is that the three names retell the corn god myth: the sheaf of barley, gathered at the annual harvest, is resown; the shield (representing a boat, bringing the secrets of agriculture, or the sun) enables the seed to grow so that it is ripe for harvest again. This cycle of life, death and rebirth is represented in the ancient folk character John Barleycorn, who was 'ploughed down' but 'got up again.' He 'grew thick and strong' but at the point of ripeness, when 'his drooping head show'd he'd begun to fail' he was cut once more, ground up, drowned and turned into beer. This process exactly mirrors the tradition of the slain king, who was killed at his peak, just before his powers began to wane and whose death restored the harvest. Beaw, Sceldwa and Sceaf were personifications of that same process, possibly even fertility gods themselves. What is most astonishing is the appearance of this tradition within the genealogy of the House of Wessex. The implication is that Alfred and his dynastic line were sprung from gods of the corn, were themselves the progeny of both Woden and an earlier corn deity who embodied the slain god tradition. One of Woden's incarnations was also as a corn god, and a 'barley-wolf' who partook of the sacred drink that, according to the tale of John Barleycorn, will 'make your courage rise.'

Carved head, probably of St Edmund, Abbey Gardens, Bury.

The next chapter will explore how such traditions persisted well into the post-conversion Anglo-Saxon period and beyond, particularly amongst rural communities. Viking pagan settlers would also have revived memories of the old gods and practices. For this reason, the response to Edmund's death amongst the communities of East Anglia stimulated both Christian and pagan folk-memories. In a primarily agrarian society such as East Anglia, fertility of the land would have been of utmost importance to its people; early traditions, particularly in relation to the god of the corn, would likely have persisted, the origins of which lay in the principles of the slain king. To reinforce the point, Edmund was perceived as a son of the Wuffinga dynasty, who claimed descent from the god Woden. One of Woden's aspects was a corn god. The cult of Woden involved participation in annual rites, led by the sacred warrior-king, to ensure the health and prosperity of the land. The people were therefore dependent on both the god-sprung king and Woden himself for a good harvest. Even in Christian times, Wednesday (or Woden's Day) was considered a lucky day for sowing and planting crops. The slaughter of Edmund yielded no practical benefit to the people of East Anglia, although the Christian payback in terms of spiritual blessings was clear. Yet if understood in the context of Woden's cult and the slain king tradition, as a sacrifice by both king and deity, the practical benefit was obvious: it ensured the fecundity of the land. When Edmund is quoted as saying 'I would rather die for my country if I need to', it can be interpreted literally. Edmund, the pure, incorrupt virgin king willingly sacrificed himself at the moment his powers began to wane, represented by his defeat in battle. In so doing, the king's regenerative spirit flooded into the East Anglian earth, ensuring the safety and prosperity of his kingdom – its lands and people – even in death. This reconciles the promise inherent in Edmund's name; 'Edmund' means 'wealth' and 'protection'. Oral culture, emerging from the needs of the people, used Celtic theories of kingship and fertility to construct Edmund's myth; these ideas were largely present in both Saxon and Viking culture and, in turn, they informed later written Christianised accounts. It also goes a long way towards explaining Edmund's associations with fertility miracles.

There are obvious parallels between the slain king and the story of Christ, and it could be argued that Christ is the ultimate expression of the slain king tradition. It is therefore perhaps unsurprising that aspects of Edmund's martyrdom echo the slain king, inasmuch as his martyrdom was an emulation of Christ's own sacrifice. Yet comparisons between Edmund and the slain king tradition go further, drawing in other myths and illustrating the extent to which the stories of saints' lives drew on earlier beliefs.

Some have noted how the motifs of Edmund's death, the severing of the head, its ability to speak, and the wolf connection, recall 'the ancient cult-war and the heroic deeds of Edmund's ancestors, and the ultimate ancestor, the wolf-god Beowulf.' Others have speculated on whether parallels exist between Edmund's execution and the ritual sacrifices of pagan German traditions. It could certainly be argued that Christian kings 'sacrificed' by violence were, in many respects, continuing earlier traditions of pagan ritual king-slaying (such as the likely ritual dismemberment of Christian King Oswald by the pagan Penda.) Ritual killings undoubtedly took place within Saxon society, and were certainly prevalent amongst Viking raiders, who practiced human sacrifice throughout Britain and Ireland. Such sacrifice was a feature of the Woden / Odin cult. Ritual killings have been identified around mound five at Sutton Hoo. Those bodies had been hanged, beheaded and mutilated, the earliest of which can be dated to 530-710, and the latest from 970-1220, spanning both pre and post-conversion eras. The assumption is the earlier burials constitute pagan sacrifices, and the later, Christian executions. But Christian burials, even if the result of executions, typically lie east-west; none were oriented in this fashion around mound five. Another suggestion is the bodies were of ideological 'deviants' who threatened established authority. They may include both executions and sacrifices, but there is very little evidence to distinguish one from another. What is most important is that 'ritual' killings, whether judicial or religious, occurred in the kingdom of East Anglia well into the period of Edmund's reign and beyond. There is little evidence for ritual king-slaying in the tradition of the slain king with Anglo-Saxon society. But, as we have seen, it was certainly a feature of Celtic and Norse society, and elements of the slain king custom firmly reside in Anglo-

Saxon concepts of kingship, royal genealogies and myths of ancestor-gods such as Woden. Edmund's death as a ritual killing cannot be discounted, nor that his death was perceived as ritual or sacrificial in nature.

An East Anglian Arthur

Whether a ritual slaughter or not, the manner of his death connects Edmund to a rich seam of Celtic, Anglo-Saxon and Norse mythic symbolism. This golden thread of elder tradition has at various points been Romanised, Christianised, Germanicised and then Christianised again. But the kernel of original truth remains intact. These mythic symbols, with their roots in prehistory, have trickled down through successive cultures, been re-imagined, yet retained and enriched.

The Danes tied Edmund to a tree, scourged him, shot him with arrows and speared him with javelins. Abbo was no doubt keen to draw comparison with St Sebastian, and he made this link explicit. But the tree reference immediately embeds Edmund in the slain king tradition, connecting the god-king to heaven, earth and the otherworld. The other obvious parallel is with Woden: In his Odin aspect, Woden was hanged from the world tree Yggdrasil for nine days and nights, pierced by his own spear, in order to learn the wisdom of the runes. Thus he was seen as a god who, by self-sacrifice, won knowledge for the benefit of man. This echo serves to reaffirm Edmund's Wuffinga heritage, as a descendent of Woden. There are further similarities with another Norse god: Balder. Balder was magically protected from any object in creation, save for mistletoe; his 'achille's heel' was a mistletoe arrow, shot by the trickster god Loki. The other gods made sport by throwing spears and darts at him, in the same way that the Danes threw spears and shot arrows at Edmund 'as if in sport'. The land was then drained of vitality as nature mourned Balder's death. Decapitation was also symbolic of the corn deity in the slain god tradition: an ear of corn was struck from the sheaf, but new growth would sprout from the head of the dead plant.

The great grey wolf found guarding Edmund's severed head is a clear allusion to the king's dynastic heritage, as a scion of the Wuffinga royal line. Wuffinga, meaning 'kin of the wolf' is a folk name, signifying a totemic affinity with the creature in question. The bearer of the name was an emblematic figure embodying the origins of the wolf-myth. The wolf protecting Edmund can therefore be seen as a kind of guardian spirit of the East Anglian dynasty, even as Woden himself. In Celtic tradition the wolf is closely associated with the horned fertility god Cernunnos and, in the lives of the early Irish saints, wolves frequently figure in the role of helpful animals. Ravens and wolves were Woden's familiars, collecting the heroic dead in much the same way as Odin's valkyries. Therefore, perhaps Edmund's wolf can also be viewed as a device for acknowledging the king's sacrifice – one that found approval in both Christ and Woden.

As mentioned earlier, it is unlikely that incoming Germanic tribes constituted an invasion or mass migration; rather, they probably arrived in small groups and settled amongst the existing populations. If there was a fundamental shift, it was in the Romano-Celts themselves, who gradually adopted new Anglo-Saxon cultural practices to express new affinities and identities. In turn, while apparently rejecting Roman urbanisation, the pagan Anglo-Saxons respected and enjoyed aspects of Celtic culture where an affinity existed. Celtic culture likely exerted some influence over the Germanic peoples in the late prehistoric period, potentially shaping later Germanic pantheons, traditions and practices. It has even been suggested that Woden / Odin has his origins in Celtic myth. There are certainly parallels between Thor and Odin, and the Celtic gods Taranis, Dagda and Esus. Anglo-Saxons and Britons probably intermarried and traded with Celtic kingdoms, their cultures cross-fertilizing through exposure to shared ideas and traditions. The Tara Brooch, for example, illustrates the impact of Anglo-Saxon art styles on Celtic metalwork. Similarly, Celtic objects such as the sceptre (as well as Byzantine and Merovingian finds) were amongst the grave goods discovered at Sutton Hoo.

Mound One at Sutton Hoo - the likely site of King Rædwald's burial.

It is unsurprising then to find that the Celtic worldview is, in fact, persistent in Edmund's story. From concepts of divine kingship and sacrifice to the evolution of the church and attitudes to nature, Edmund's myth illustrates the influence and continuity of cultural memory from Celtic through to Anglo-Saxon and Viking.

Celtic human sacrifice, for instance, included shooting victims with arrows, or impaling them, much like Edmund's ritualized death. But the main area of association lies in the symbolism of the severed head, which in Celtic culture was venerated as the seat of the soul and capable of displaying magical powers. It also had associations with kingship.

This reverence manifested itself in the heathen cult of the head and continued into the lives of Celtic Christian saints.

Irish tales tell of how King Cormac mac Cuilennáin's severed head was a sage of poetry, learning and government and continued to look after its people when the king was dead. Similarly, King Bran's head reputedly protected his territories against plague and invasion.

The legend of St Melor describes how the saint was murdered, reputedly in 411; he was decapitated, and the assassin carried St Melor's head on a journey to visit the saint's wicked uncle. En route, the murderer grew thirsty and St Melor's head commanded the man to fix his staff in the ground, from where a spring miraculously gushed forth. Later, St Melor's body and head were buried on Mount Arat, some distance apart. The body rose up of its own accord to reunite itself with the severed head.

Another tradition from France concerns the sacred springs of Alesia, venerated by the Celts in pre-Christian times. A legend of a martyred saint became associated with one of the springs: decapitated by her betrothed in the third century, St Reine's head struck the ground and a healing well came forth, known thereafter as the Spring of Sainte Reine.

A comparable legend is linked to the Welsh St Lludd. Upon being beheaded, her head rolled down a hill and rested against a rock, from where a spring of pure water immediately gushed forth.

Similarly, when Edmund's head was found between the paws of the grey wolf and retrieved by his people, a miraculous freshwater spring broke through the soil where the head had lain. Near Hoxne in Suffolk – one possible site for Edmund's martyrdom – is a deep moat enclosing a small island on which the very same freshwater spring was said to be found. This spring 'the occupiers of the field have never been able to divert'. The ill and infirm journeyed there in the Middle Ages for healing.

Celtic-style stone heads have been found built into Danish churches, suggesting reverence for the head was maintained into the medieval era in Denmark. It is tempting, therefore, to speculate that Edmund's Danish executioners threw his head into thick brambles to avoid the possibility of supernatural revival, and to deny his kingship-in-death.

The restoration of Edmund's head with his body, leaving a line akin to a red silken thread around his neck, is echoed in the tale of Sir Gawain and the Green Knight. One interpretation of the Green Knight's complex and contradictory nature is as a dying and rising vegetation god; this is a view that fits well with Edmund's embodiment of the slain king.

Alongside miracles of fertility, Edmund's other primary saintly function was as protector of the land and the people, hence the epithet 'shield of the East Angles.' The Anglo-Saxons would not have been exposed to the Arthur myth as we know it today, yet an interpretation of Edmund's story through the prism of Arthurian lore yields some interesting lines of enquiry. Arthur was a sun god of the British Celts, a patron of agriculture in its early form. Edmund too was compared to the sun in prophecy. In Celtic coin art depictions of the sun are accompanied by stalks of grain, illustrating how the fertility of the land is blessed by both the sun and rightful sovereignty. The supernatural birth of Arthur reveals him as a 'saviour' or national champion. Aspects of

Arthurian legend also allude to the underlying philosophy of the slain king: during their quest for the Holy Grail, Arthur's knights encounter the Fisher King – or maimed king – one in a line of grail keepers. He suffers from a wound that does not heal, and exists in a condition of dead-aliveness in the Grail Castle; as a result of his imperfect state, the kingdom has turned to a wasteland. He can only be healed if answers to a series of questions concerning the grail can be answered. Percival, one of Arthur's knights, cannot answer these mystical questions and remains at the Grail Castle. Yet he perseveres and is finally successful. In the 1981 movie Excalibur, Roger Corman expands the mythos by providing the self-evident answer to the question: what is the lost secret of the grail? The answer is: the land and the king are one. The mystery at the heart of the grail is service, by the kingdom to the king, and by the king to the land.

Slain in his last battle by his treacherous nephew Mordred, Arthur is carried off by his sisters in a barque to the mystic isle of Avallon or Avallach, 'the Place of Apples' (potentially Glastonbury), in the Western Sea. There he remains, awaiting the fateful day when Britain shall require his aid once more. The parallels between Arthur's role and Alfred's declaration of Edmund as England's first patron saint are clear: they are both national champions, intimately bound up with the land. We shall see later how various landscape features within the kingdom of East Anglia correspond with Edmund's kingship, further reinforcing the link between the health of the land and Edmund the slain king's procreative energies.

The story of Edmund's martyrdom then is a continuation of an established Celtic, Anglo-Saxon and Norse tradition. It is a tradition that reconciles Christian and pagan beliefs, pagan enriching Christian, but Christian never quite achieving absolute dominance. Edmund's ritualized death is like a reflection on water: first it resembles a thoroughly Christian martyrdom, then shimmers, becomes indistinct, and is revealed as Woden tied to the world tree, pierced by his own spear; then it suggests Baldur, the subject of target-practice for the sport of others; then Edmund becomes the sacred sacrificed king of early pre-Christian tradition – a bridge between worlds and restorer of vitality to the land; he is an embodiment of the corn god, of fertility and renewal. Again, in sainthood Edmund resembles the archetypal holy martyr at first glance. Yet his reputation for fertility and revenge mark him as a kingly sentinel of Arthurian tradition, Woden's avenging son Widar, and an embodiment of both willing sacrifice and mythic hero. In his slain god aspect, Edmund even compares with Osiris – the dead king who continues to be powerful, even in death.

If the notion of Edmund the holy Christian king epitomizing a thoroughly pre-Christian mythology seems odd, consider the following: St Botolph, the patron saint of travelers and traders, was born in 615. 64 ancient churches were dedicated to him, the majority in East Anglia. Yet he also thoroughly exhibits critical aspects of the slain god tradition. He is associated with good weather and abundant harvests. In a mirror of Halfdan's fate, where his body parts were distributed to other tribes, St Botolph's body was exhumed, divided into thirds, and sent to three abbeys, including Westminster. Parts of his corpse ended up at Bury abbey.

St Wulstan of Bawburgh, who died in 1016, was another East Anglian saint, although little known. He was a layman, neither monk nor priest, and was associated with guardianship of a holy well at Bawburgh. Wulstan was revered as a protector of farmers and was later denounced as a 'god of the field', a clear allusion to his role as a Christianised corn god. Saints were local expressions of the needs, behaviours and attitudes of a community, absorbing the traits of pagan heroes and gods as necessary. In Anglo-Saxon East Anglia it is clear from examining the characteristics of its saints that the agricultural corn god was a significant force. Edmund was not alone amongst East Anglian saints in embodying its mysteries, but he was certainly the region's greatest example of the sacred, sacrificed king.

of Britain's history of belief. So is the parallel observation, or merging, of different religious practices. Invasions occur, kingdoms are conquered, practices are outlawed or fall out of fashion, but no one belief holds absolute sway over the minds of the people. History is messy, and the body of lore and tradition in a community, at any point, is a complex weave of the disparate, and sometimes contradictory, beliefs that went before.

Indeed, the dualism that exists today between Christianity and 'paganism' was itself not so pronounced in the past, as aspects of Anglo-Saxon culture reveal. And 'paganism' itself was probably a grassroots hotch-potch of local practices, lacking any substantial authority or priestly hierarchy.

Polytheistic Rome was, for a time at least, extremely tolerant of multi-faith practices; indeed, one reason for the Roman Empire's expansion and success was its integration of native deities and religious practices. For example, the Celtic divinity Belenos 'The Shining One', was regarded as a local incarnation of the Roman solar god Apollo. Within Celtic and Romano-British belief, Jesus was perceived as another incarnation of the solar god. Christianity, although in principle not tolerant of polytheism, was flexible enough to incorporate many pagan traditions into its own ritual works. An obvious example of this is Christmas. In the fourth century, a Christian writer described how:

It was a custom of the pagans to celebrate on the same 25 December the birthday of the sun, at which they kindled lights in token of festivity. In these solemnities and revelries the Christians also took part. Accordingly when the doctors of the Church perceived that the Christians had a leaning towards this festival, they took counsel and resolved that the true Nativity should be solemnized on that day.

An identical approach addressed the use of pagan sacred sites. In a letter to Abbot Mellitus, Pope Gregory the Great provided instructions for Augustine, head of the Catholic mission to Britain in 597 AD:

…Tell him what I have long gone over in my mind concerning the matter of the English: that is, that the shrines of idols amongst that people should be destroyed as little as possible, but that the idols themselves that are inside them should be destroyed. Let blessed water be made and sprinkled in these shrines, let altars be constructed and relics placed there: since if the shrines are well built it is necessary that they should be converted from the worship of demons to the service of the true God, so that as long as the people do not see their very shrines being destroyed they may put out error from their hearts and in knowledge and adoration of the true God they may gather at their accustomed places more readily.

Perhaps the best-known example of dual-faith observance lies with Rædwald, Anglo-Saxon king of East Anglia and overlord to the other English kings. In his personal temple was set up one altar to Christ, and another to his preferred heathen deity – most likely Woden – upon which sacrifices were made. For polytheistic pagans, this worship of multiple deities was perfectly normal, but no doubt deeply frustrating for the Christian mission. Based on Gregory's guidance, the Christian strategy was to tolerate pagan traditions. Rather then eradicate them, they sought to Christianise such practices - spells became blessings and the attributes of pagan heroes were migrated to saints. This weaving of pagan and Christian produced a rich and idiosyncratic Anglo-Saxon church. England evolved into a truly sacred land, peppered with shrines, holy wells, springs, parish churches and pilgrimage routes. Following William of Normandy's invasion, the Normans were amazed at the extent to which even the most mundane places were revered as sacred; every village seemed to have its own saint and holy place.

St Gregory's Church Rendlesham, the probable location of Rædwald's dual faith altar.

Christianity arrived in Britain with the Romans, brought by traders, settlers and the military in roughly 180 (although the legend of Joseph of Arimathea establishing a church at Glastonbury puts the date as early as 63AD.) Christ was worshipped in a pluralistic, polytheistic Anglo-Roman society, alongside Roman, Celtic, Greek and other deities.

But prior to Roman invasion under Claudius in 43AD, Celtic society was dominated by Druidic belief. Likely to have been well established in Britain by 600BC, theirs was a fundamentally animistic religion; in other words, the Druids believed the natural world was imbued with spirit. Birds and animals held sacred, totemic significance. A complex pantheon of deities, many of which were local, were worshipped. Chief amongst these were the Great Mother goddess Dana, Ana or Anna, and her consort Belenos, Beel or Bile, a solar deity and dispenser of light and healing. Celtic deities were often personifications of nature and, in many cases, actually embedded in rivers, streams, lakes, trees, hills and mountains. Two cults were of particular importance in Celtic life: the cult of the horned god representing fertility, and the cult of the head, already discussed, representing divinity and otherworldly powers; the very seat of the soul. This powerful and active cult was found throughout the Celtic world. We have seen already how parts of Edmund's myth can be traced back to these Celtic origins.

Druids were priest-rulers, aristocrats attached to a royal household as a shaman, advisor, law-giver, teacher and prophet. Although the Isle of Anglesea – the seat of Druidic power in Britain – was comprehensively destroyed under Roman occupation, Celtic paganism continued to be practiced in rural areas (Christianity was an urban religion.) Pliny mentions that Druids were still very numerous in Britain in 79AD. It is likely their traditions became absorbed into Romano-British practices, stepping out of the natural temples of oak, ash and yew and into man-made environments, in imitation of the Roman model. At Cavenham, near Bury St Edmunds, a number of ritual objects have been found, indicating that priests did indeed continue to practice the old religion in parallel with the incoming Christianity. The temples themselves were part of a 'tradition of sanctity', originating in the Iron Age but continuing into Roman occupation.

England did not become officially Christian until 313, following conversion by the Emperor Constantine. Yet Christianity failed to make significant inroads in Britain under Roman rule. There are various reasons for this: a decline in the economy and ongoing environmental deterioration would not have endeared the official Imperial religion to the pagan populace. Also, Britain likely escaped the decree of Emperor Theodisian in 391, banning the practice of paganism. Heathen elements continued to creep back into Christian practices because of a lack of doctrinal authority; a Celtic pagan revival was active, at least in rural areas, in the late 3rd century. Romano-Celtic burials of the period show evidence of decapitation, reflecting the ongoing Celtic reverence for the head as the seat of the soul; in some cases this type of burial continued well into the Anglo Saxon period. All in all, following the Roman withdrawal, the church began to crumble and the old beliefs took hold once more.

Celtic Church, Roman Mission

Despite the waxing and waning of Christian influence under Roman occupation, the period saw an emergence of a new form of Christianity peculiar to Britain. Then as now, there were many churches, many 'flavours' of belief operating under the aegis of Christianity. The Celtic church was one of them, and was itself likely a heterogeneous mix of practices throughout Ireland, Wales, west and northern England, and Scotland. It arrived in Britain in the late fourth century, rooted in the earlier traditions of nature, learning and locality. Theologically, a key difference was the assertion that the world and humanity were essentially good, rather than fundamentally sinful as argued in Roman dogma. There were other differences too. It has been suggested that, based on some key similarities between the Druidic religion and Christianity (the belief in descent from one god, in an afterlife, in moral rectitude), Druids took on the mantle of priests and monks as Christianity gained greater footholds. The Celts, it has been claimed, insisted on the primacy of direct, personal experience of supernatural realms. This requirement informed the evolution of Celtic Christianity, leading to the development of unique practices separate from, and at odds with, Roman Catholic doctrine. What these esoteric traditions might be is a subject for debate. If aspects of Druidic practice did surface in

Celtic Christianity, they may have been limited to attitudes to nature, women, marriage amongst the priesthood and the tonsure – which, in contrast to Roman Catholic edicts, was a shaved area at the front of the head running from ear to ear – a supposed Druidic device. Yet at the Synod of Whitby the Celtic tonsure was denounced by the Roman delegation as the 'tonsure of Simon Magus' – a thinly veiled charge of heresy, associating the Celtic Christians with, at best, gnostic tendencies and, at worse, sorcery. To add fuel to the fire, the Britons did not deny it. It has been speculated that this silence hints at a form of esoteric Christianity within the Celtic Church; a body of secret wisdom of which only a select few were custodians.

To further enforce the link between Druidism and the Celtic Church, stories of early saints' lives clearly merged both pagan and Christian elements. St Brigit, for example, was raised in the house of a Druid, associated with fertility and sun worship, and was depicted in such a way as to be aligned with the pagan Great Goddess – in both her Earth Mother and Triple Goddess aspects. Certain miracles associated with Celtic saints were inherited from the pre-Christian Celts' veneration for water, and the cult of the head. St Patrick's later chroniclers exaggerated his apparent supernatural powers, depicting him as a spell-caster and druidic wonder-worker. And the emergence of ninth and tenth century poems with Celtic hermits as their subject matter also reinforced the image of nature-lovers who enjoyed an almost druidic mystical relationship with birds, trees and animals.

The Celtic Church appeared to believe that the Saxons were unworthy of any missionary efforts, and so British Christianity failed to penetrate the pagan Anglo-Saxon kingdoms of East Anglia. Centuries before these Germanic tribes arrived in Britain, they were venerating an ancient fertility goddess known as Nerthus. In parallel with Celtic worship of the solar god Bel and earth goddess Dana, Tacitus in the first century AD, describes how Nerthus 'intervenes in human affairs and goes on progress through the tribes' in a consecrated wagon, pulled by cows and accompanied by a priest. Nerthus was one deity of the *Vanir* cult, the old religion of the Germanic people whose chief representatives were Freyr and Freyja. It is thought that aspects of the Vanir cult were brought to England in some form, and maintained in folklore until relatively recently: in 1598, a harvest celebration occurred near Eton whereby an effigy supposed to depict a corn goddess (Ceres or Nerthus) was crowned with flowers and carried on a wagon, accompanied by men and maid-servants. The range of harvest celebrations – corn dollies, harvest queens, festivals and last-sheaf ceremonies – were part of this tradition and practiced until well into the 19th century. May rites, performed after seed time in rural cultures, featured an elected 'king' and 'queen', sporting an oak and hawthorn wreath respectively, to oversee proceedings. This 'marriage' echoed the pre-Christian symbolism of the union of sun and earth, male and female, Belenos and Dana.

Anglo-Saxon pagan migrants would have encountered a variety of beliefs on their arrival in Britain: Celtic Christianity, Romano-British and pre-Roman Celtic paganism. As outlined above, native British paganism bore many similarities to its Germanic and Scandinavian counterparts, given that the former likely influenced the latter; this goes some way towards explaining why certain places of sanctity show continuity of usage, in some cases from prehistory forward.

Where there is evidence of cultural continuity, so too is there evidence of continued use of places of earlier sanctity by the Anglo-Saxons; they reworked prehistoric monuments into the fabric of their culture, and used them as boundary markers, burial sites, moot-places, church sites and *cwealmstows* or killing-places. These sites of pre-Christian power continued to hold meaning even after the conversion. Like their Celtic precedents, Anglo-Saxon pagan worship seems to have taken place in open-air sanctuaries. Indeed, their use of hills and open spaces may even have been an expression of ongoing Romano-Celtic beliefs. If Anglo-Saxon settlers and Romano-Celts had intermarried, this would certainly have been possible. At Heslerton in the Yorkshire Wolds, for example, archaeology has discovered a Late Roman, or earlier, rural shrine complex linking a spring to a well-head. This ritual complex, which appears to have been the site for seasonal gatherings, had been maintained throughout the life of the Anglo-Saxon settlement, implying continued usage.

The Germanic Vanir cult, which spawned the fertility goddess Nerthus, was eventually superseded by the gods of the Æsir, a pantheon well known today. From place name evidence, it appears that at least four of the Æsir gods were venerated in Anglo-Saxon East Anglia: Woden, the chief deity, Thunor or Thor, Tiw or Tyr, and Frigg. Although often perceived as an aspect of the Norse god Odin, Woden was a distinct figure with his own character and purpose – especially as the father of Anglo-Saxon kings. His cult was restricted to the south and east and enjoyed its apogee in the seventh century. A number of metalwork finds in East Anglia depict a horn-helmeted man, probably Woden, and point to his veneration in the region; the objects may well have been employed as talismans. Belief began dying out by the eighth century, but he was not forgotten. Originating in the Rhineland, Woden was thought to be a storm god and a god of war, poetry and magic, with power over the dead. He was also leader of the Wild Hunt, processing his homeless dead across the sky. In an entry in the Anglo-Saxon chronicle in 1127, the Wild Hunt was allegedly observed at a deer park in Peterborough: 'many people saw and heard the huntsmen in full cry. They straddled black horses... while their hounds were pitch black with staring hideous eyes.' Woden was an aristocratic deity. In Hárbarðsljóð – one of the poems from the Old Norse collection known as the Poetic Edda – Woden 'owns all the gentlefolk that fall in fight, but Thor the thrall-kind.' In other words, Woden was the god of kings and nobles, Thor the god of serfs and the working class. As such, Woden had a key role amongst the Anglo-Saxon dynasties; he was the ultimate ancestor, from whom all kings were descended.

Although often perceived as an aspect of the Norse god Odin, Woden was a distinct figure with his own character and purpose – especially as the father of Anglo-Saxon kings. His cult was restricted to the south and east and enjoyed its apogee in the seventh century. A number of metalwork finds in East Anglia depict a horn-helmeted man, probably Woden, and point to his veneration in the region; the objects may well have been employed as talismans. Belief began dying out by the eighth century, but he was not forgotten. Originating in the Rhineland, Woden was thought to be a storm god and a god of war, poetry and magic, with power over the dead. He was also leader of the Wild Hunt, processing his homeless dead across the sky. In an entry in the Anglo-Saxon chronicle in 1127, the Wild Hunt was allegedly observed at a deer park in Peterborough:

'many people saw and heard the huntsmen in full cry. They straddled black horses... while their hounds were pitch black with staring hideous eyes.' Woden was an aristocratic deity. In Hárbarðsljóð – one of the poems from the Old Norse collection known as the Poetic Edda – Woden 'owns all the gentlefolk that fall in fight, but Thor the thrall-kind.' In other words, Woden was the god of kings and nobles, Thor the god of serfs and the working class. As such, Woden had a key role amongst the Anglo-Saxon dynasties; he was the ultimate ancestor, from whom all kings were descended.

The Pope himself ultimately intervened to make Christian inroads into pagan Anglo-Saxon territory. Pope Gregory the Great dispatched a mission from Rome in 597. Led by Augustine, its express purpose was to convert the Saxons, and to address the lack of Roman church authority in Britain; up to that point the church was a patchwork of different practices. Landing on the south coast, King Æthelberht of Kent received the party and allowed them to settle at Canterbury. The mission wasted no time and, in fact, was extraordinarily effective in its efforts. According to a letter from the Pope, over 10,000 English were baptized in what amounted to a ten-month period. Rædwald the Bretwalda was amongst the Saxon aristocracy who succumbed. He was baptized in Kent in roughly 604, perhaps even at the invitation of Æthelberht. However, as we have seen, Rædwald was only partially committed to the new religion and kept two altars at the royal town of Rendlesham – one dedicated to Christ, the other to Woden.

Despite his status as figurehead of the Saxon pagan pantheon, Woden himself was ultimately integrated into the Christian worldview. In royal genealogies, as Woden became increasingly removed from the more sinister associations with witchcraft and sorcery, he was at the very least tolerated by the church in his role as father of Saxon kings – as a means of validating their power and authority. We have already seen how the mythical lineage of the House of Wessex was extended beyond Woden to incorporate the likes of Noah and Adam. And in the Nine Herbs Chant text, a 10th century charm for the treatment of poison, Christ and Woden are linked; Christ is the wise hanging Lord who created the powerful curative herbs to defeat evil. Woden received the wisdom of the nine herbs and used them to conquer the serpent. In the same way that Christ stood over the 'malignant ones', so Woden destroyed an evil force with Christ's gift of herbs.

The Anglo-Saxon poem 'The Dream of the Rood' is a clear illustration of how pagan themes were used to enrich the Christian vision. The poem, dating from roughly 1000, recounts Christ's crucifixion from the perspective of the tree used to fashion Christ's cross. Christ is a Germanic hero, a warrior-king, and the blurring of cross and tree draw comparisons between Christ and Woden, who hung from the world tree to obtain the secrets of the runes. There are further parallels with the Norse god Balder. These ambivalent depictions of Christ in Anglo Saxon texts illustrate the persistence of heathen traditions, and their popularity; pagan songs and poems were even favoured by monks.

The East Anglian Church

Sigeberht was a son of the great king and overlord Rædwald, and he did much to accelerate the progress of Christianity in East Anglia. His efforts were given support by Felix, a Burgundian priest who arrived in East Anglia as part of the ongoing Gregorian mission. Despite his apparent Roman allegiance, Felix was steeped in Celtic Christianity, coming from a Frankish monastery originally established by the Irish missionary Columbanus. Sigeberht endowed a bishopric to Felix at *Dommoc* (most probably Dunwich or, alternatively, Walton Castle); Felix was ordained by the Archbishop of Canterbury, Honorius, in 630. A second bishopric was founded at Elmham, and King Sigeberht established a monastery for his own use at Beodericsworth (later to become Bury St Edmunds) in 633.

A second purely Celtic mission to East Anglia came in the form of Irish monk and mystic Fursey and his brothers Foilan and Ultan. Sigeberht welcomed them and endowed land at *Cnobheresburg*, or Burgh Castle, the old fortress of the Roman Saxon Shore, for the establishment of an abbey. From there, Fursey ministered to the East Angles and attained considerable popularity. So much so that, after choosing a hermit's life of quiet contemplation, the numbers that continued to visit him were so great that he fled to France in 644.

Of the two missionaries, Fursey was given prominence by the eighth century Anglo-Saxon chronicler Bede as the only missionary working in East Anglia. Bede was fond of the Celtic Church and prone to comparing the golden age of Celtic Christianity's mysterious early missionaries, such as Aiden and Cuthbert, with the corruption of his own day; perhaps this explains Felix's omission. Although Sigeberht was tolerant of the both the Roman and Celtic traditions, the fledgling East Anglian church at least in part emerged from distinctly Celtic Christian origins. Fifty years later, Botolph shored up the faith by establishing a minster at *Icanho* or Iken, a few miles from the Wuffinga royal town of Rendlesham. This approach of establishing minster churches enabled the religion to reach out to a widely distributed rural population.

The stone cross at St Botolph's Church Iken.

St Botolph's Church, Iken, site of the original minster.

Sigeberht eventually abdicated his kingship and chose a monkish life at the monastery he founded at Beodericsworth. When a Mercian army attacked East Anglia, his people begged him to lead them into battle, but he refused. In desperation, his army dragged him from the monastery, but still Sigeberht would not take up arms; he went into battle carrying only a staff. Unsurprisingly, he and much of his army were wiped out.

The East Anglian church's influence waxed and waned following Sigeberht's death as power shifted from Christian to pagan, East Saxon to Mercian rulers. Religious change was, after all, a top-down affair and, at the grass roots, Christian and pagan would have likely continued to co-exist for generations. While the attitude of a typical pagan Saxon towards Christianity is hard to discern, a number of factors would have shaped their decision to convert, or not. First of all, people would have been reluctant to discard their local myths and traditions – the very stories that defined them and their sense of belonging and entitlement. These traditions inevitably involved myths and rituals based on their deities and heroes. People would have also feared revenge from the old gods; the risk of failed harvests or division from their ancestors in the afterlife, would have been real concerns. Only when a tipping point or conclusive act has been realized would the population be able to submit to conversion with impunity. Such a game-changing event may have occurred at Goodmanham, just outside York, and site of a great temple, probably to Woden. As recounted by Bede, in 627 the high priest of the temple, Coifi, desecrated his own altars and shrines:

He formally renounced his empty superstitions and… set out to destroy the idols. Girded with a sword and with a spear in hand, he mounted the King's stallion and rode up to the idols. When the crowd saw him they thought he had gone mad, but without hesitation, as soon as he reached the temple, he cast a spear into it and profaned it.

It certainly appears as though the priest's actions testify to his Christian conversion. There is one possible alternative explanation for this however: the priest may have been a disciple of Woden, observed in the act of destroying an earlier temple dedicated to Nerthus. The act of spear-throwing may have echoed the behaviour of Germanic pagans, who threw spears over their enemies, dedicating their destruction to Woden.

The changing nature of burial rites, normally providing hints of conversion in a region, are inconclusive in East Anglia. Cremation, for instance, was a feature of some, but not all, pagan burials. Records show 141 Saxon cemeteries in East Anglia, of which 75 are in Suffolk; the rest can be found in Norfolk. Yet of 5,900 cremations recorded in East Anglia, 86% were in Norfolk, leaving 843 in Suffolk. This perhaps only tells us that inhumation was a preferred burial rite in the south for both pagan and Christian burials, and cremation cannot be used as an indicator of conversion.

The location of burials provides better evidence. Unlike the Celts that preceded them, the Anglo-Saxons re-used ancient prehistoric and Bronze Age monuments, either for burials or group gatherings, possibly as a way to establish links with the past and legitimise their presence. Sutton Hoo itself has revealed usage stretching back to antiquity: a Bronze Age palisade and Neolithic ditch have been discovered, along with filled-in ditches from a Celtic field system.

But as Christianity crept across Saxon territories in the seventh century, these sites became perceived as unholy; burials were brought into the heart of a settlement, whereas previously cemeteries were located at the periphery. There are examples of this at Bury, where three Anglo Saxon cemeteries have been discovered within the town. It does not necessary follow that sites such as Sutton Hoo were discarded; rather, their function changed. Still retaining their powerful spirit of place, they became the focus of other activities, possibly of ritual killings and criminal or 'deviant' burials. Even in the face of Christianity's powerful influence, the Wuffinga kings of East Anglia still sought to retain their links with pagan Scandinavia, if only to assert an air of legitimacy in the face of threats from both across the North Sea and from Mercia in the west. One line of thought suggests that the famous epic poem Beowulf was authored in East Anglia in the reign of the Wuffinga King Ælfwald (713-749), to explicitly establish a link between the Wuffingas and the legendary king of the Danes.

Earth Mothers And Counter-Magi

By the end of the seventh century, the Anglo-Saxon kingdoms were officially Christian. But the pendulum of belief swung away from Christianity under Danish pagan occupation. Despite the Viking leader Guthrum's nominal conversion to Christianity, the church suffered, and its organization was shattered. Crowland Abbey in the Fens was burned down. Further destruction may have been suffered at Bury St Edmunds, Ely and Soham. Iken, Brandon and Burrow Hill were abandoned. Without any ecclesiastical authority in the region, it is certainly possible that both Danes and Anglo-Saxons returned to heathen practices in some shape or form. Only later in the tenth century was the bishopric of East Anglia restored and monastic life revived at Bury. There is no doubt that many ecclesiastical buildings were sacked and burned or abandoned in the period, but there is also evidence for some remaining untouched, and worship continuing.

Guthrum's conversion did lead to much of the Danelaw being Christianised. However, Christian Viking still attacked Christian, and Viking paganism was not moribund. The Danish position was more likely to be *halbgloubig* or 'half-believing', seeking the benefits of Christianity without abandoning their old religion; there were, for instance, distinct advantages in adopting Christianity in terms of trade and the offering of mercenary services. Some opportunistic Danes even sought annual rebaptism in order to acquire baptismal gifts and clothes from their sponsors.

Magic and superstitious folk practices continued throughout the period and beyond, despite possibly fatal consequences. By the tenth century, a fearsome judicial system was in operation; places of execution would have been an everyday sight for both town and country-dwellers. The laws of Cnut expressly forbade the worship of heathen gods, sun or moon, fire, flood, water, wells, stones or trees, and outlawed witchcraft and sorcery. Such an edict would clearly not be necessary unless the forbidden practices were continuing. Old traditions died hard; the ghosts of heathen deities were embedded everywhere, from place names to days of the week, and could not be easily forgotten. Further examples of pagan tradition reside in literature from the period: The 'Dream of the Rood' makes reference to *wyrd* – a specific Anglo-Saxon pagan term relating the weaving of men's fate or destiny by three supernatural sisters. It also appears in the epic tale of Beowulf. The Old English Maxims, or poems, describe the powers of Christ as great, but fate (or wyrd) as stronger. In Bald's Leechbook, compiled in the early 10th century, a magical remedy for protection against elves and goblins is provided. In the early 11th century, Wulfstan, Archbishop of York, delivered a fire-and-brimstone sermon for which he was famed known as 'The Sermon of the Wolf to the English.'

In it he denounced the many sins of the English, and claimed that Viking incursions were punishment for their godlessness. Amongst the many subjects of his wrath were sorcerers and witches, although the word used to describe the latter was *wælcyrie*, which translates as 'valkyrie' – the Norse chooser of the slain. Quite how or why valkyries were operating in the midst of the English is unclear.

One clearly pagan practice that did gain Church sanction when Christianized and documented in the 11th century was Æcerbot, or Field Remedy. The day-long ritual, used to fructify underproductive fields, was a complex affair. Four turfs, removed from each corner of the field, were nourished with a particular 'porridge' and taken into a church, where four masses were performed over each. The turfs were then returned to the field. A plough was anointed with a certain oil mixture and set in motion. The ritual invoked 'erce, erce, erce, Mother of Earth' ('erce' being either a ritual cry or the name of an unknown earth goddess.) As the plough cut its first furrow, the priest incanted:

Hail to you, Earth, Mother of Mortals, may you grow big in God's embrace, filled with food for the use of humankind.

The whole affair echoes Celtic belief, the priest channeling the power of God / the sun into the plough, which then penetrated and fertilized the earth, representing the archetypal marriage of male and female, sun and earth. The earth goddess references hark back to Nerthus and Celtic Dana. Use of the practice illustrates how, even in the later Saxon period, fertility and harvest were major preoccupations, particularly amongst rural communities.

Folk magic was conducted into the medieval era, particularly in rural areas. What is perhaps surprising though is the overt participation by the Church. The annals of the Abbey of St Edmunds describe a curious fertility ritual, known as the Oblation of the Bull, which was practiced in at least the 13th century and continued into the Tudor era. It is explicitly linked to the cult of St Edmund. A white bull, kept by the abbey in the area of meadowland known as the Haberden, was made available for any married woman who wished to conceive. Led by a monk, the woman accompanied the bull, which was adorned with garlands of flowers and ribbons, through the streets to the west gate of the abbey. Inside she would proceed to the shrine of St Edmund and make an offering, then pray for a child, kiss the shrine and retire. The procession was always accompanied by singing monks and a large congregation of townsfolk. The bull was treated exceptionally well: properly fed, never yoked to the plow or baited at the stake. The rite occurred on St Edmund's primary feast day of 20th November, reinforcing the link between the saint and his surprising powers of fertility. It is a ritual with clear pagan, and likely Celtic, origins. The Druidic culture-god Hu was described as 'a bull dwelling in a sacred stall.' There is also some evidence to suggest that white oxen were used for ritual Druidic sacrifice. They were magical animals, and certainly sacred, being associated with the Otherworld. In parts of England and Scotland, until quite recently, small herds of white cattle were preserved, echoing this earlier Druidic requirement.

The role of saints, Edmund included, was critical in the Church's battle to win the hearts and minds of those who remained staunchly pagan. In a sense they functioned as counter-magi, or Christian magicians. The church realized that, if it was to ultimately gain converts, it would need to stop complaining about pagan wizards and begin addressing the needs that these magicians fulfilled. Alongside priests, monks and bishops, saints played a key role in this. Saints were part of the process of Christianising an otherwise heathen animistic worldview; they inherited the attributes of pagan heroes and deities in the same way that a church became holy by locating it upon a site of pagan sanctity. Old traditions, sacred wells, springs, trees and stones, became absorbed into the broader Christian story. Saints also provided a useful way in which the divine could be made intelligible in the world; they were a physical, localized expression of Christian virtues. Wondrous aid could be sought by praying before the shrine, kissing or touching relics, drinking or eating from objects where relics had been in contact, making offerings or procuring objects, bones or material that were somehow connected to the saint. A certain Norman individual apparently successfully crossed a dangerous ford on account of a relic from the shrine of St Edmund that he carried with him.

Despite the church's rejection of heathen polytheism, the cult of saints itself became a pantheon of demi-gods. Faith in their powers spread across all society, from knights and nobles to priests and peasants. A specific saint was available for every locale and to address every ill. This diversity only helped drive the popularity of their veneration, with each saint characterised by idiosyncratic folk rituals and practices.

It is unsurprising then that, in the midst of this complex cultural weave, the golden thread of elder mythic symbolism is maintained. We have seen how religious beliefs in Britain were respected and honoured by successive waves of immigrants. The story of Edmund reflects this. It incorporates essential notions of divine kingship, threads of Celtic and Germanic customs, Christian traditions, folk practices and superstitions. Even in an overtly Christian society, heathen beliefs persisted, not just amongst the laity but also the Church. This was, in fact, a deliberate tactic, recommended by the Pope himself, and one which informed the character of British and English Christianity.

VILLA REGIA, AXIS MUNDI

The Cursus And The Villa

Edmund is both an historical and a mythic figure, an archetypal hero who battles through life, achieving greatness and, in death, becomes eternal. At a mythic level, his final resting place is a significant component of the overall legend. The hero's residence or grave is a symbolic point from which the flow of life is released into the land. Its physical locus represents the world-navel, the omphalos, the centre of the world or *axis mundi*, the tree of life, the sacred womb or the cosmic mountain.

Where the hero has died and passed back into the void is a place marked as sacred; it is a symbolic shrine and altar, a locus of healing, fertility, sanctuary and meditation. Towns and cities are often built around this shrine, from which paths to the four cardinal points unfurl. In both pagan and Christian Anglo-Saxon culture, the burial place of a king was extremely holy; his life-force and *mana* continued in death and blessed the site of his burial. The cosmology of medieval Suffolk was such that Edmund's shrine existed at the centre of an imagined symbolic landscape, one that was alive with meaning; the land was dynamic, sacred and valued.

Some observers have suggested that Edmund's early veneration, prior to his translation, was part of a tradition of sanctity with its roots in pre-Christian practices; it is claimed that Edmund's first shrine at 'Sutton' was located in an area of pagan worship, and his cult emerged from that heritage. Whether or not this is the case, it merits similar discussion in relation to Bury St Edmunds. There are hints that the town, and the location of Edmund's shrine within the abbey church, possess a sanctity maintained over centuries. Like Edmund's myth, the story of Bury St Edmunds is a golden thread that can be plotted back to prehistory.

Generally assumed to have little or no history prior to Anglo-Saxon settlement, there is in fact evidence for activity or settlement in Bury stretching back to the Neolithic. The town's sanctity is hinted at in geographic alignments and place names, and confirmed in its medieval sacred geometry. Edmund's shrine was certainly the physical and symbolic centre of medieval Bury. The town's growth and success was entirely a function of Edmund's cult. If his body had not been relocated to Bury (or Beodericsworth until 925), Sigeberht's humble monastery would likely not have become such a powerful institution. Pilgrimage and royal patronage enabled the abbey to prosper. Without Edmund, the town's evolution would have been very different.

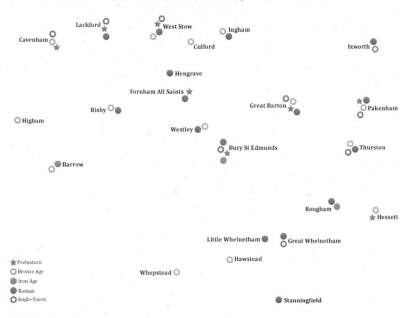

Distribution of archaeological finds near Bury St Edmunds.

Bury's ascent began in 633 when King Sigeberht founded that same monastery. What the town consisted of prior to that event is not known. We cannot know whether it was little more than a backwater, a small and insignificant settlement, or something more. If it was a place of no particular note, it is reasonable to wonder why Sigeberht chose to locate a monastery – one he intended to make use of himself – in a place of no particular importance. Bury was nowhere near the royal town and Wuffinga power-base of Rendlesham, nor was it in the vicinity of the two bishoprics at Dunwich and Elmham. It was also some distance from Ely (where St Augustine may have founded a Christian community) and Soham (where Saint Felix is thought to have founded a monastery.) Perhaps, after all, some form of earlier status or sanctity commended the location to Sigeberht and his Celtic Christian bishops.

Bury's strategic importance may have been identified early on, thanks to the River Lark which runs through the town. Along with the River Gipping and Great Ouse, it could have forged a navigable corridor between South Lincolnshire and the North Norfolk coast, settlements in Breckland and those around the Icknield Way, Bury and the Sandling settlements towards the southeast. Bury was positioned at the approximate halfway point between the eastern edge of the Fens and the Orwell estuary – a useful waypoint.

East Anglia was one of the most populous areas of Britain, even in prehistory. There is evidence for early human settlement, or at least activity, in and around Bury. Flint tools have been excavated in the town, along with Bronze Age pottery and Celtic and Roman coins. Pakenham and West Stow were the sites of Neolithic and Mesolithic settlements respectively. Bronze Age tumuli have been identified at Westley, less than a mile from Bury, as well as Risby, Barrow and Pakenham; a large Bronze Age barrow – the Hill of Health – was discovered at Culford, and Thurston is the location of Bronze Age cremations. A possible Bronze Age tumulus within Bury itself was utilized as the site of a Saxon court.

Perhaps one of the most important indicators of Bury's potential antiquity is Fornham Cursus, located in the village of Fornham St Martin roughly two miles from Bury centre. About 50 cursuses have been found throughout the UK, generally constructed around 3-2000 BC. Their original purpose is unknown, but they do tend to conform to certain arrangements, which help suggest their use. Most occur near rivers, with one end closer towards water – encouraging speculation about 'sacred river' rituals. Cursuses are also often found within more extensive ritual landscapes, near to henges (earthen bank and ditch rings), and with internal features such as post holes or standing stones. There is some limited evidence of burial or cremation, usually at one end only, but very little in the way of artifacts. Orientation and the objects they align to appear to be as important as the cursuses themselves, almost as though they functioned as giant landscape signposts. 64% point to either a prehistoric site, or an ancient church (itself potentially the location of an earlier sacred site.) The best-known and most extensive examples are at Stonehenge, where the cursus measures 1.7 miles, and the Dorset Cursus on Cranborne Chase, running for six miles. In addition to the example at Fornham, there are a number of other possible cursus in the region.

Theories of their purpose include processional or ritual paths, or spirit-ways; the enclosed nature of these earthworks may have functioned as a *cordon sanitaire*, restricting the movement of potentially dangerous ancestral spirits to the area within the earthwork. Their placement close to rivers also echoes the folk belief that spirits could not cross flowing water. Further, geophysical analysis of the West Kennet Avenue at Avebury, a wide path running 1.5 miles and flanked by stone uprights, shows that the ground was compacted *outside* the avenue. In other words, crowds attending ritual ceremonies were not allowed access to the interior pathway, which may have been the preserve of priests or spirits of the dead.

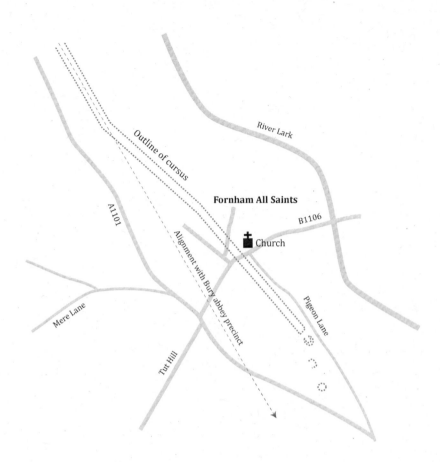

Fornham cursus. Showing alignment of the most northerly section with Bury Abbey.

The Fornham Cursus is clearly identifiable from crop marks and comprises three straight lengths, each at slightly different orientations. Potentially the lengths were built at different times, as is believed to be the case at other cursuses where changes of direction occur. The northernmost terminus has not been located, but the southern one is visible from the air and next to a circular crop-mark. The village church actually sits on one section. A local spur of the ancient Icknield Way may have continued on to Bury and, if so, it could have forked near West Stow, following the path of the River Lark. If this were the case, the trackway would have passed very close to Fornham Cursus.

Perhaps significantly, the northernmost section of the cursus in aligned to the abbey complex at Bury St Edmunds. With its axis extended it would pass through, or very near to, the abbey precinct. Whether this is by accident or design is open to debate, but if the abbey grounds were the site of earlier ritual significance then this alignment becomes important.

Rising 30m above the cursus, one mile to the southwest, is Tut Hill. Previously assumed to derive from 'Teut' or 'Toutates', the chief divinity of the Druids, nowadays 'tut' is thought to denote a hill of observation, from the Old English *totian*. Although possibly not a location of Druidic significance, Tut Hill certainly looms over the village below, providing high ground from which to survey the cursus landscape.

Roman and Iron Age finds have been located in many villages surrounding Bury. The closest recorded Roman archeology to the town is Eastlow Hill near Rougham. It is the last survivor of the Four Hills, a line of Roman burial mounds from the second or third century AD, standing beside Eastlowhill Road, an extension of Peddar's Way. The surviving mound was excavated in the 1840s, revealing the skeleton of a man in a lead coffin, in a brick lined burial chamber. The Four Hills were probably the burial place of a family who lived in a nearby villa, discovered at about the same time. Great Whelnetham is the site of a number of Roman finds, including a spear, sacrificing knife, vessels and coins. The village may have been a Roman station, or alternatively a burial site for a disputed villa at Bury.

Although there is little evidence currently of Roman settlement in Bury, there has been speculation that it may have been the location of one 'Villa Faustina'. There is reference to such a villa in the Itinerary of Emperor Antoninus Pius (Faustina being his wife); when she died, Antoninus sought her deification, so any such naming of a Roman station may simply have been in her honour. Alternatively, the name may have referred to the seat of an individual named 'Faustinus', or may even have derived from 'faustus', meaning fortunate, prosperous or pleasant. In this instance Villa Faustina would simply have meant 'happy town'. Others have suggested that the commander of the 14th Legion had his Praetorium, or officer's quarters, here. Further speculations have focused on earthworks in the Haberden – the area between the River Lark and Southgate Street – being of Roman origin, though there is no evidence for this.

A Roman votive figurine, depicting the god Mars, was found in the town, and in 1783, four carved stone heads were unearthed, lying facedown, beneath the foundations of St Edmunds church. While some argue these heads are medieval aborted carvings of Edmund, others suggest they may be of Roman origin, depicting Roman deities.

Another possible claim for Bury's early strategic function lies in a proposed Roman road linking the Icknield Way, which passes west of the town, with the Peddars Way, which runs to the east. The road would have run through Bury, to the north, providing a waypoint for moving goods and communications between these two major ancient trackways, and potentially for switching between land and water-borne transport at the point of intersection with the Lark.

Bedericsgueord

There is some confusion regarding Bury's status in the Anglo-Saxon era, due to a lack of consistency in the use of its name. In documents from the period, the town was variously referred to as *Beadoriceswyrthe*, *Beadericeswirde*, *Beoderic-weord* and *Beoderici-cortis*, which translate as the enclosure, turn or bend, villa or court of Beoderic, Beoderic being presumably the ancient lord of the town. Compilers of abbey registers seem to prefer this interpretation, but there is another. An earlier spelling, used by Abbo in his *Passio*, *Bedewic-gueord* or *Bedericsgueord*, can be interpreted as 'the town that has authority of pre-eminence in prayer', denoting a superior place of worship; 'bederic' signifies prosperous, happy and pleasant – the same as 'faustus' is Latin. It is tempting to speculate on what, if anything, made ancient Bury a 'superior place of worship' and a 'fortunate town.' Perhaps these references hint at earlier sanctity and continuity of worship, pre-dating the town's Anglo-Saxon development; others have suggested as much.

What is more certain is Bury's status as an Anglo Saxon royal town – a *Villa Regia*. Abbo confirmed this status in his *Passio*, and Bede noted that Saxon royal towns were generally placed on the sites of Roman stations (thereby supporting the claim for Bury's Roman settlement.) It is likely that Bury achieved *Villa Regia* status around the time that Sigeberht established his monastery. As ecclesiastic houses go, it was a small affair, and populated by secular clerics: four priest and two deacons, who were not subject to the rigid rules of an order. They made no vows and were free to marry, arrangements perhaps suggestive of a Celtic Christian influence. Edmund's body was not translated to the monastery immediately following his death; this did not occur for another 34 years. Assuming the killing-place was Bradfield St Clare, five miles from Bury, the decision to move the body makes sense. Edmund's cult grew rapidly and no doubt ambitious churchmen saw an opportunity to exploit his popularity. Also, the monastery perhaps offered a degree of protection, from the Danes in particular. As a Villa Regia, Bury was a place of some status and it would have been an entirely appropriate location for an East Anglian king's final resting place.

A new church, probably a round wooden structure, was built within the monastery grounds to house Edmund's remains. This firmly established the link between Edmund and the town, resulting in the monastery growing into a major pilgrimage centre, so much so that the town changed its name in 925 to St Edmundsbury. King Æthelstan was the monastery's first likely royal patron, followed by Edward I. In 945 Edward bequeathed an area of land, known as the *banleuca*, to the monastery. The *banleuca* extended well beyond the monastery's own grounds and, later on, the abbot enjoyed almost total autonomy within its jurisdiction – no clergyman could celebrate mass or erect an altar without his permission. Its boundaries were marked by four crosses: the Virgin's Cross, Eldhawe Cross, Black Cross and Weeping Cross. The octagonal base of the Virgin's Cross survives today.

The Danish King Cnut, son of Sweyn – famously the object of St Edmund's wrath – was another benefactor. In 1020 he commanded thirteen monks from St Bene's to colonise Bury, led by Uvius – Bury's first abbot. A new stone round church was built and consecrated in 1032 by Archbishop Æthelnoth 'in honour of Christ and St Mary and St Edmund.' The refounding of Bury's religious house as an abbey was a significant step forward.

Edward the Confessor visited Bury Abbey in 1044 and made more endowments in addition to the *banleuca*. These included over eight full hundreds and one half-hundred in West Suffolk (a 'hundred' was an area of land encompassing one hundred 'hides' or

The Great Axis alignment, viewed from the Norman Tower.

households.) A Saxon court was held on Thing Howe (literally: 'assembly at the hole'), a hill to the north of Bury surmounted by a tumulus, and the area became known as the Thingoe Hundred. Eventually the entire land endowment was referred to as the 'Liberty of St Edmund'. King Edward made a further grant to the abbey in 1065, including permission to establish a mint.

Pre-Conquest Bury was little more than a single road, a north-south street, represented by Northgate St and Southgate St today, which ran parallel to the River Lark. Excavation of the bowling green in the modern Abbey Gardens shows this road passing through the abbey precinct. Mustow St, forking at a right angle to the main north-south axis, may also have been significant – its name implying the location of a Saxon 'muster' or meeting-place. At this time, the town's market was located at the junction of Westgate St, on the site of St Mary's Square.

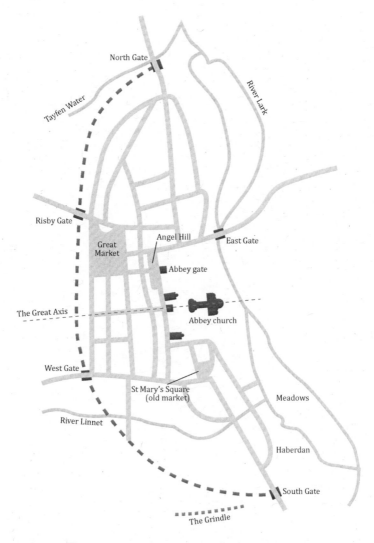

Plan of Bury St Edmunds, showing the town's defensive walls and line of the Great Axis.

As the abbey grew, so did the town. In 1086 there were 342 houses in the town, with a population including: 30 priests, 28 nuns, 75 'poor people' such as millers, brewers and cooks, and 34 knights.

Bury's defences were a mix of wall, river and earthwork. Five gates spanned the town, each accompanied by a chapel to Our Lady and each with a constant flame burning. Bury had only one defensive wall on its western side, which extended from Westgate to Northgate. The area around Tayfen Water (a stream running from the Lark, now long since vanished) in the north, and around the River Linnet to the south (in the area known as the Haberden), were protected by earthworks – banks and ditches. An ancient earthwork known as the Grindle also ran due west from Southgate Street. A second line of internal earthworks, referred to as Cnut's Ditch, marked the perimeter of the abbey from Mustow Street to St Margaret's church on Angel Hill, but this may have been for the purposes of drainage rather than defence; modern speculative depictions of the medieval abbey show this ditch functioning as a moat, with bridges providing access to the abbey itself.

King Edward's personal physician, Baldwin, a French monk from Saint Denys, was made abbot in 1065. His contribution to the status of the abbey was substantial. Baldwin organized the reconstruction of the abbey church into a grand Romanesque building, beginning with the east end. In 1095 the body of St Edmund was moved to its new home, and work continued until 1140, including construction of many of the abbey's other monastic buildings.

Bury's Sacred Symbolism

Baldwin's programme of improvement also extended to the town, conceiving a plan according to symbolic principles. The original north-south axis, known classically as the *cardo*, was later accompanied by an east-west axis, the *decumanus*, forming a crucifix. Baldwin introduced two parallel streets – Abbeygate and Churchgate Street – which bounded a medieval grid of streets that still survives today. Churchgate Street was the Great Axis, an alignment extending through the archway of the Norman Tower, towards the church's west front, along the knave and terminating at the shrine of St Edmund. This axis conforms to the mythic conception of a town or city, where the body of the hero lies enshrined at its centre, within a sacred *temenos*. The shrine functions as a symbolic locus, a world-navel from which the hero's wellspring of life-force flows. It has been observed that the Great Axis may be an echo of ancient straight-line traditions from earlier civilizations. In Damascus, a similar alignment extended into the sacred precinct of the temple of Zeus, which later became a Christian church and then the Grand Mosque. Within was a shrine containing the reliquary of John the Baptist. Churchgate Street's alignment with the abbey precinct and shrine of St Edmund is an equivalent that perhaps suggests continuity from before the founding of the abbey.

The symbolic nature of Bury's layout was not restricted to the abbey however; it also extended to the rest of the town. Bury's town plan reflected a medieval interpretation of the entire universe. At its heart was the shrine of St Edmund, the 'Holy of Holies', with the abbey that surrounded it representing Heaven. Outside the abbey's boundary was

the realm of the angelic host, still known today as Angel Hill. Beyond was the secular town, laid out as a grid of roughly 163m-long sections, but with key alignments such as the Great Axis still connected to the upper realms, representing the path to salvation. Finally, beyond the town's perimeter – its walls, ditches and rivers – lay Hell.

Angel Hill, Bury St Edmunds.

The abbey's expansion continued under Abbot Anselm, who built St James's Tower, now known as the Norman Tower, at the point on the Great Axis that separated the abbey from the outside world.

Abbot Sampson completed the abbey church's spectacular west front, using stone from as far away as Caen, adding a great central tower and lower octagonal towers to either side. He also improved the accommodation, including a new hall and the Black Hostry, to house the abbey's visitors. The abbey church became one of the largest in Europe, measuring over 500ft in length and with a west front 250ft across.

At its height, Bury abbey contained 80 Benedictine monks, a score of chaplains and over 100 servants and retainers. As well as one of the most popular pilgrimage destinations in England, it was a centre of artistic splendour and culture, with a rich library and frequent contacts with the University of Oxford. Such indulgences were made possible as a result of the enormous wealth it generated. It is estimated from documentary evidence that over 700 monasteries were founded in England. Bury abbey was the fourth richest. By the twelfth century, the town was an established and successful community, and the hub of East Anglian religious and commercial life; along with Ipswich it was the most dominant town in Suffolk. The landed estates of the abbey dominated the region, consisting of 300 separate holdings in Suffolk, Norfolk, Essex and elsewhere. The town's

One of three great arches on the west front of Bury's abbey church, now a private dwelling.

annual fair was one of the greatest in England, attracting clothiers and merchants from across Europe. No other market existed within six miles, reflecting the town's advantage and control in the area.

St Edmund's shrine remained the Abbey's fundamental wealth-generator, his status as a local embodiment of archetypal hero-king resonating with pilgrims from across Britain and Europe. The focal-point of the entire town's symbolic layout was his shrine, located behind the abbey church's high altar, upon a marble block, flanked by the relics of other saints: Jurmin, Botolph and Humbert, plus the skull of St Petronella, which bestowed cures for headaches and the ague. The bones of King Anna – another East Anglian regent - and his son, Jurmin, were also kept in the church.

The area in the immediate vicinity of Edmund's shrine was considered extremely holy, so much so that Richard I approached the shrine barefoot and prostrated himself before it. It was a liminal place where different rules applied, being both a sanctuary for those seeking protection, and a place in which miracles and healing occurred. A pardon bowl absolved anyone who drank from it of 500 days of sin, while sick pilgrims were offered holy water from the saint's cup, which they drank in three sips. Water may have been sourced from a well or fountain in the crypt directly beneath the shrine; the 15th century chronicler William Worcester observed that there was a 'very fine spring of water' within the chapel of St Mary *in cryptis*. Springs were venerated as places of healing and fertility in pagan cultures. For Celts, they were the focus of cult practice and ritual, organized around certain deities and water-spirits.

The shrine itself consisted of gold plates decorated with coloured precious stones, surmounted by a canopy. Powerful, sacred objects surrounded the shrine, including Edmund's warbanner, sword, mail shirt, plus the banner of the Emperor of Cyprus. Four candles burned continuously at each corner of Edmund's shrine, at considerable cost.

Thus, the whole of Bury town was imbued with sacred symbolism. A pilgrim travelling to observe the saint's feast day of 20th November would approach through Suffolk's rolling frost-bitten countryside, spying the abbey church's towering spires, and columns of smoke from the stalls of St Edmund's fair. Passing one of four crosses to mark the perimeter of the *banleuca*, he marks the walls and ditches that define the town's boundaries; one earthwork called the Grindle makes clear the land beyond the town is the realm of demons; the lair of man-eating beasts. Entering via one of five gates, the pilgrim briefly visits the accompanying chapel to Our Lady, making an offering for the upkeep of the perpetual flames that purify the portals between the town and the outer world. Within, the busy main streets lead inexorably to the great abbey, defining the town's main geomantic axes. He follows a ragged line of travelers, from peasants to mounted nobles, passing stalls selling everything from spices to silk. They stop briefly to watch a ribald mystery play, but continue on, leaving the profane world behind. Crossing a second portal, through St James's bell tower, the pilgrim enters the abbey precinct. The magnificent church is ahead, its great bronze doors shimmering in the low winter sun. Beyond this final portal lies some of England's holiest ground. He passes beneath the great arches of the west end, into the low light of the nave; the interior is thick with incense and lit by guttering rushes. The noise and press of the crowds fade, now a world away. Shafts of sunlight, piercing the smoke at the far end of the church, signal the location of St Edmund's shrine. In silent reverence, he passes thirteen great stone capitals before reaching the church's transepts, where lay brothers stationed before the east end beckon the penitent forward. Finally, in humbled awe, the pilgrim enters the holy sanctuary and circles the ambulatory where the golden shrine of St Edmund reveals itself, sat upon fine marble and encrusted with gems, illuminated by four candles, perpetually lit. Whispered entreaties, weeping and prayers can be heard as supplicants reach out to press their hands and lips against the place where St Edmund's incorrupt body rests. In this most sacred of places, where the veil between Heaven and Earth is thinnest, the pilgrim kneels and makes his appeal to the holy king and martyr, glory of East Anglia and protector of all England.

Bury's construction as a sacred town is by no means unique; Bristol, Carmarthen, Canterbury and others all contain elements that represent certain geomantic principles or sacred configurations. But Bury provides an exceptional example of a town that conforms to the notion of a mythic city, organized as an elaborate temple with divisions between sacred and profane. At its heart lies the shrine of the hero-king, the holy precinct or *temenos*, a focal point for access to the otherworld; it represents a wellspring of vital energy for the community.

THE KINGDOM OF EAST ANGLIA

The King And The Land

The fundamental truth of the slain king myth, found in Anglo-Saxon notions of sacred kingship and embodied in the story of Edmund, is the revelation that the king and the land are one. The regent's kingship, his ability to rule, his moral rectitude, his health and vitality, were intricately linked to the fertility of the land and the wellbeing of the kingdom. That relationship became explicit in death, when his body was, in some cases, literally divided up and buried across the kingdom to ensure a good harvest. His death released both his own life force, and that of the divinity he represented, back into the land he presided over as ruler.

The conception of Edmund's kingdom amounts to a complex relationship between the lived environment, landscape, cultural and social forces. It is a worldview difficult for modern sensibilities to understand. To solve this problem, the Dreamtime of Australian Aboriginal tradition is often cited as a contemporary example of that same complex interrelatedness displayed by earlier cultures. In this cosmology, almost every topographical feature of the landscape has a deep resonance. The country is laced with dreaming tracks, and sacred totems, through which people interact with threads of mythic memory, tracing the routes of mythic personalities and events as they walk the land. It could be argued that, up to the Reformation and even the Industrial Revolution, rural populations in England regarded the landscape in this way. Medieval communities were certainly intimately connected to the landscapes around them. The magical worldview of the Anglo-Saxons and Danes would have perceived Prehistoric sites, ditches, trackways, earthworks and natural features as part of a mythic landscape narrative. Edmund was a critical component of that narrative, his presence weaving through the kingdom and confirming his authority over the land in both life and death. The connection between the land and kingship is further enforced by language. Kings, as conduits for divine energies, were expected to deliver straight and true judgments; correct behaviour, reflected in proper and truthful speech, was a sign of royal legitimacy and upheld the very nature of sacred kingship. This relationship can be found in etymological links between words relating to kingship, morality and straightness. The Indo-European root words *reg* and *rect* mean 'movement in a straight line' and have parallels in Old High German, Old Celtic and Old Saxon. Words derived from these two roots in relation to ideas about space include: region, rectangle, regular and direction. In relation to morality, words include: correct, right, righteous and rectitude. In relation to kingship, some example words are: regal, regency, reign, realm, royal and rule. 'Ruler' is a crossover word with a dual meaning, referring to both the exercise of government and straightness or measurement. Taken as a whole, the combinations of meanings, derived from the original root words, describe kingship in relation to both the regent's status as *ruler* and his moral *rectitude*, as well as geographic *regions* that were subject to his government. Once again, the king and the land are intimately linked, this time in language.

The association extended into specific parts of the landscape. Kingship and moral rectitude were expressed as straightness in the form of boundaries, roads, borders and alignments. Examples of straight paths as symbols of imposed order can be found in Roman roads, Chinese urban geomancy and, indeed, the rectilinear layout and main cardinal axes of Bury St Edmunds. A line of royal burial rounds in the Kilmartin valley in Argyllshire, for instance, is another powerful symbol of kingly authority. Bible references also link straight paths with divine kingship and righteousness.

Rivers, drainage ditches, moats and ancient parish boundaries all contribute to a vast network of ditches across Suffolk, such that Abbo described the Kingdom of East Anglia as 'water-girdled'. It is generally assumed that the southern boundary of the kingdom was defined by the River Stour, but it is also possible that the rivers Lark and Gipping marked it, forging a navigable corridor between Bury and Ipswich. If this were the case, Bury would have been situated at the very edge of the kingdom.

St Edmund's connection with the land was confirmed by the naming of a mini-shire, bequeathed to Bury abbey by Edward the Confessor, as the 'Liberty of St Edmund'. As mentioned previously, it consisted of over eight full hundreds and one half-hundred in West Suffolk. The area to the east was divided into the Liberty of St Etheldreda in the north, and The Geldable in the south. The Geldable, a small region of eleven hundreds, was the only area of Suffolk subject to direct taxation by the king's sheriff.

The Hundreds, recorded in Domesday Book, were created in the middle of the tenth century after East Anglia, as part of the Danelaw, had been reconquered by the West Saxon kings. A 'hundred' was an area of land encompassing one hundred 'hides' or households. Boundaries between hundreds can still be found today in the broad-ditched Hundred Lanes. The most spectacular surviving example in Suffolk divides Bosmere from Hartismere and is 'as impressive as any landmark of its kind in England.' Its route as a trackway, flanked either side by formidable ditches, can be seen best winding east from the A140 – previously a Roman road – at Little Stonham. Another impressive Hundred Lane runs north past the western boundaries of Earl's Green, Wyverstone and Westhorpe, still bounded on one side by a great hedge.

The best example of Edmund's kingly qualities described in landscape form is Devil's Dyke, also known during the period as Holy Edmund's Fortifications, or Edmund's Dyke. As well as providing defence, it demarcated the western edge of both the Kingdom of East Anglia and the Liberty of St Edmund. A series of three dead straight ditches measuring 7.5 miles in total, Devil's Dyke is a potent and lasting testament to Edmund's divine kingship, moral rectitude and ability to rule. It's function as both a physical boundary and a means of defining sovereignty and kingdom is also reminiscent of Celtic traditions. We have already seen how Edmund was described as an ideal ruler and model king. The Devil's Dyke, functioning as both linear earthwork and boundary line for Edmund's kingdom, is perhaps the ultimate expression of the link between a perfect king and his land.

1: Parham	8: Lothing / Mutford	14: Stow	20: Risbridge
2: Loes (with Woodbridge)	9: Wangford	15: Bosmere-and-Claydon	21: Thingoe (with Sudbury)
3: Plomesgate	10: Blything	16: Ipswich	22: Thedwastre
4: Wilford	11: Hoxne	17: Samford	23: Bury St Edmunds
5: Carlford	12: Hartismere	18: Blackbourn	24: Babergh
6: Coleness	13: Thedling	19: Lackford (with Exning)	25: Cosford
7: Lothingland			

The East Anglian Hundreds, showing the division of hundreds into the Liberty of St Edmund, the Liberty of St Etheldreda and The Geldable.

The Great Ditches

The Devil's Dyke forms part of a line of impressive East Anglian frontier defences, in places as deep as eighteen feet and with a width of seventy-five feet. They are oriented northwest to southeast, and run southwest from the Fens in a staggered formation, typically with a ditch to the west and a defensive earthwork to the east. The ditches cut across the ancient Icknield Way, and were likely constructed to block or control access to the trackway, or to defend the East Anglian plain on its most vulnerable aspect, in conjunction with the defensive line of the River Stour. King Penda subjugated the East Angles in the mid seventh century, despite the presence of some or all of these great ditches. Thereafter, the need for a strong defensive bulwark against attacks from the west would have been acutely recognised. There are at least eight ditches in total. The westernmost earthwork is Dray's Ditches, on the northeastern outskirts of Luton. Other ditches can be found further east, but the most easterly site in the Icknield Way alignment is Black Ditches at Cavenham Heath, just south of the point where the Way crosses the River Lark.

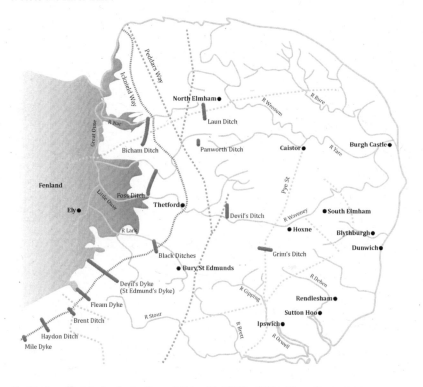

The Kingdom of East Anglia, showing the great ditches, Icknield Way, Peddars Way and major rivers.

It is generally thought that the dykes were created at the end of the Roman occupation, based on pottery and coin finds at Devil's Dyke, dating it to the late fourth century. However, there is a possibility that some were constructed on earlier Prehistoric sites. The westerly ditches – Dray's Dyke, Ravesborough and Deadman's Hill Dyke in particular are associated with major concentrations of barrows on prominent ridges, suggesting a relationship with those earlier Bronze Age monuments.

Suffolk's Hundred Lanes.

Devil's Dyke is the longest of the series of ditches, running from the clay plateau of the Cambridge-Essex border to the Fens. Extending across Newmarket Heath to woodland near Wood Ditton, Edmund fought the Danes here, one of the two armies possibly making use of the ditches, in 903. Some have also suggested it is the site of Boudicca's final battle between the Iceni and Roman fourteenth and twentieth legions. The dyke is magnificent feat of engineering, considering construction of the entire earthwork occurred simultaneously, and was not altered or enlarged thereafter.

Fleam, or Balsham, Dyke is roughly seven miles southwest of Devil's Dyke and curved in places. It commences at Fen Ditton and runs parallel to the Balsham Road, segmented at its mid-point by the A11. At Mutlow Hill – a Bronze Age barrow – it crosses the route of the Icknield Way. Mutlow Hill translates as 'Moot Hill' – a place of Anglo-Saxon assembly, and is similar in its toponymy to Bury's Mustow Street. Nineteenth century excavations discovered remains of a possible Roman ceremonial building. The ditch marks four parish boundaries: Great Wilbraham, Fulbourn, Balsham and West Wratting.

Brent, or Pampisford, Ditch is the shortest of the Cambridgeshire Dykes. The name

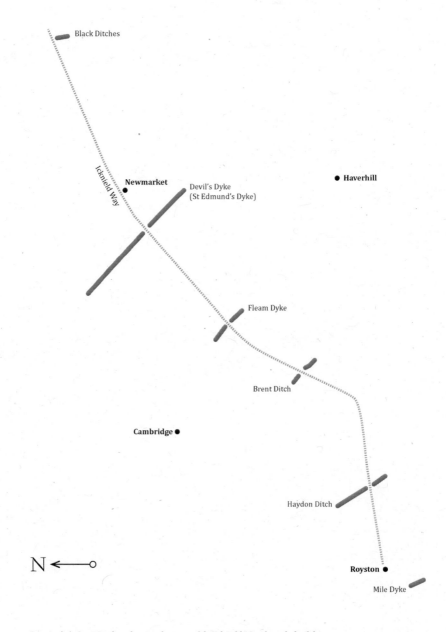

Black Ditches

Icknield Way

Newmarket

Devil's Dyke
(St Edmund's Dyke)

Haverhill

Fleam Dyke

Brent Ditch

Cambridge ●

Haydon Ditch

N ←—○

Royston ●

Mile Dyke

East Anglia's Great Ditches, showing the route of the Icknield Way through the dykes.

Brent here means 'steep'. Although the defensive bank has been leveled, the ditch remains deep in places.

Bran or Heydon Ditch runs from the end of the Essex Plateau at Heydon to Black Peak, in between Fowlmere and Melbourn. At the Heydon end it is 122m above sea level, at Black Peak only 24m. The ditch is severely damaged, much of it levelled by farming. Excavations revealed fifty Saxon-era decapitated or dismembered bodies. The skeletons were all mature males, save for two likely females and one newborn. Interpretations suggest this section of the ditch, which marks a change in orientation, was an execution place, where victims were killed and then buried. They may have been criminals or 'deviants', comparable to the deviant burials at Sutton Hoo. The bodies faced eastwest, suggesting a Christian-era site. Even so, these liminal places may have retained an association with Woden in his aspect as god of the hanged. The ditches represented boundaries between not just geographic places, but the mundane and spirit-worlds too. The linear earthwork in the form of a cursus at Fornham All Saints has already been discussed. Dating from up to 3000BC, its use is unknown but is unlikely to bear any deliberate correspondence with the themes of kingship outlined in this chapter, unless utilized by later cultures for those ends (if anything remained to make use of.) However, the fact that one section is aligned with Bury's abbey precinct hints that Edmund's shrine was a location of ancient sanctity, possibly in relation to the the freshwater spring once found there.

Suffolk is riddled with geological and man-made depressions in the form of moats and grundles or grindles. Grundles – the name is unique to East Anglia – are very deep hollow ways with steep banks rising to 5.5m in places. An earthwork called 'The Grindle' ran due west from South Gate, just outside Bury's walls. Other examples can be found at Wattisfield and Stanton. The former terminates in a pond; the latter, running for half a mile, at the corner of a field. There is a link in the use of 'grundle' or 'grindle' to denote these deep ditches with the monster Grendel from the epic poem Boewulf:

Grendel was the name of this grim demon
Haunting the marches, marauding around the heath
And the desolate fens;

As already mentioned, it has been suggested that Beowulf was authored in East Anglia in the reign of the Wuffinga King Ælfwald (713-749), to explicitly establish a link between the Wuffingas and the legendary king of the Danes. Grendel was a monster that resided in low-lying watery places. Marshlands and bogs were dangerously deceptive, seemingly safe on one hand but able to drag the unfortunate down to the Lowerworld – the land of the dead (and also a place of wisdom.) 'Grendel' is connected to the Old Norse term meaning 'to bellow' and later the Middle English term meaning 'angry'. An East Anglian dialect word 'grindle', means 'drain' or 'ditch'. Thus, in the same way that aspects of kingship were linked to certain landscape features, so Grendel's monstrous qualities were linked to border-places such as pits, bogs and ditches. The Suffolk village of Grundisburgh may bear the same origins; an Iron Age fort at nearby Burgh was reputedly haunted by marsh-dwelling demon. St Botolph's bones were brought to the church built on top of the fort in order to exorcise it.

Ancient Trackways

Rivers, drainage ditches, moats and ancient parish boundaries all contribute to a vast network of ditches across Suffolk, such that Abbo described the Kingdom of East Anglia as 'water-girdled'. It is generally assumed that the southern boundary of the kingdom was defined by the River Stour, but it is also possible that the rivers Lark and Gipping marked it, forging a navigable corridor between Bury and Ipswich. If this were the case, Bury would have been situated at the very edge of the kingdom.

Running alongside, and occasionally through, East Anglia's great earthworks are its ancient trackways. There are a number of 'St Edmunds' Ways' across the region, further linking Edmund's kingship with the landscape. Pilgrims originally used these green lanes en route to Bury abbey. One such example, in this case known as The King's Road or King's Highway, traversed the 40 or so miles from Dunwich to Bury. Originally a Roman road, it incorporated multiple dead-straight lengths of track. Later it became a popular pilgrimage route to Edmund's shrine. Although now disappeared, the road once again hints at Bury's Roman or pre-Roman origins, and Edmund's kingly rectitude expressed in straight landscape features.

The oldest of the region's trackways, the Icknield Way, follows a chalk line laid down over a period of 35 million years. It curls from the North Norfolk coast, through Hertfordshire to join the similarly ancient Ridgeway, a ninety-mile long track from Buckinghamshire that terminates in Wiltshire, near Avebury. Animal migration routes would have followed the chalk ridge initially, followed by human trails later.

The way is not thought to be a single track, but a skein of parallel paths. It is 'a braid of stories and memories, passing out of the known and into the mythic'. In East Anglia the way is particularly ill-defined, branching off in different directions and following many spurs leading to areas of local importance, potentially including a route into Bury.

Its original purpose is generally thought to be a trade route, connecting England's early industrialists at Grimes Graves in East Anglia with primitive farming communities in the west. There are hints that these trackways had uses beyond the mere transport of goods. Some were perhaps ritual procession-ways; others, spirit-lines that connected sacred sites, or provided passage for the souls of the dead. The Icknield Way would have been used for centuries, by Romans and later as one of the four Royal Roads of England. It may even have described the southern axis of a great nation-spanning road defined by King Belinus, the fifth century legendary king of the Britons.

At Cambridgeshire, the Way intersects the great ditches, including Devil's Dyke, suggesting it was still widely used into the Anglo-Saxon period, to the extent that defences were needed to control access into East Anglia. Further west it crosses the River Thames at Goring, then proceeds through Berkshire. At this point the trackway forks: a more southerly route, in the form of the Ridgeway, passes close to some of England's finest ancient earthworks – Segsbury Castle, the Uffington white horse and Wayland's Smithy – before the Icknield Way reconnects with it in Wiltshire. Why two trackways would run in parallel like this is unclear. It is possible that one route was for summer travel, the other winter. Alternatively, the Icknield Way may have been a trade and migration route, while the Ridgeway was a ritual procession-way reserved for pilgrimage.

Bury's Roman Road. Showing the speculative route of a Roman road linking the Icknield Way and Peddars Way, and passing through Bury.

The Way finally terminates in Wiltshire, becomes the Ridgeway and passes the eastern flank of the great ritual landscape of Avebury. This area was undoubtedly southern England's most important Neolithic religious centre, and would have drawn pilgrims from East Anglia and further afield. The complex includes an enormous stone circle enclosing an area of 28 acres, and Silbury Hill – the largest artificial hill in Europe. While the Icknield way runs to the west of Bury, the Roman Peddars Way passes to the east. Although commencing in the same area in north Norfolk, their functions were ultimately different. The former facilitated trade, but the latter had a military purpose. Nevertheless, their similar starting-points may suggest that both the Peddars Way and Icknield Way incorporated a ferry linking North Norfolk with the East Lincolnshire coast. The northern end of the Peddars Way also terminates very close to Seahenge, hinting that perhaps the route had pre-Roman origins and a ritual function.

Peddars Way is one of two main northsouth roads in the region. It served Melford, Ixworth and Knettishall, while Pye Street linked Coddenham with the north and south. A network of roads was established across the entire country following occupation, enabling efficient communication, and the transport of troops, exports and products. In addition to the Peddars Way, England's main arterial routes at that time were: Watling Street, linking Dover and London to Wroxeter; Dere Street, passing from York to Durham and across the border to Newstead in Scotland; and the Fossway, running southwest from Lincoln to the south coast of Devon.

As outlined previously, a possible route for a Roman road connecting the Icknield and Peddars Way may have passed through Bury. The road approximately followed the line of the A14 from Kentford to Ixworth, weaving through, or just north of, Bury. Later, the road would have forked south to provide a route directly to Bury Abbey and the shrine of St Edmund.

A third significant trackway in the region is The Puddingstone Trail. Yet its existence is contentious, and it may not even be a trackway as such. In 1949 Dr Ernest A. Rudge discovered an alignment of large 'puddingstone' boulders, so-named because of their composition: flint fragments and sediment compressed millennia ago by glacial shifting, and resembling large plum puddings. In the absence of quarried stone, these boulders would have been highly prized amongst the communities of early East Anglia. They vary in size from those small enough to be lifted, to giants of megalithic proportions.

Following Rudge's original discovery of just five conglomerate boulders, his search expanded to 125. The route plotted by these stones runs roughly parallel to the Peddars Way, beginning at Snettisham and passing close to Castle Acre, North Elmham, Grimes Graves, Brandon, Thetford, Pakenham, Hessett and Kersey, before sweeping west past St Albums, Chesham, Thatcham and on to Avebury, following the route of the Icknield Way.

The role of the stones themselves is primarily as waymarkers, being apparently regularly placed in short, straight sections. Sixteen stones were found in the vicinity of Saxon churches, as foundations or churchyard monoliths. Some may have had earlier ritual significance. Like the Icknield Way, the Puddingstone Track seems to incorporate various local spurs, including one at Coton near Cambridge. Around Bury there are forks from Great Livermere to West Stow, Ixworth to Thurston and Ingham to Timworth and Fornham St Martin.

Rudge believed the function of the track was much the same as the Icknield Way: as a trade route for flint from Grimes Graves, with the Puddingstone Track serving additional communities further south. Yet the very existence of a trackway has been questioned by those who believe the puddingstones were deposited naturally by glaciers. Critics argue that Rudge simply plotted a route through this random distribution of erratics, ignoring those that did not conform to his trackway route. It is true that there are very few actual pathways between boulders so, in many cases, no track exists and only the stone markers are present. On the other hand, some boulders have probably been moved by human hands and placed at significant locations – fords, crossroads and churches. Whether

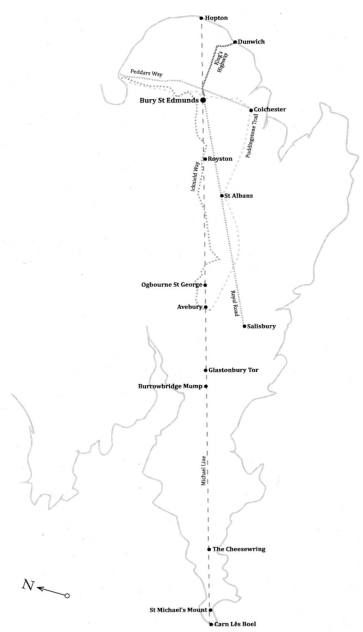

Bury's relationship to the Michael Line, Puddingstone Trail, Icknield Way, Peddars Way, Royal Road and King's Highway.

all boulders have been deliberately placed to form a coherent trackway is a matter for further discussion.

The final set of trackways fall into the category tentatively called 'visionary' or 'mythic' landscapes. While not existing as physical pathways, they align places of sanctity, memory and mythic resonance, and are most commonly encountered in the form of 'ley lines'. These mythic tracks have a sort of parallel existence, weaving in and out of their physical incarnations. In this sense they perform a function similar to Aboriginal songlines. The key question, outside the scope of this book, is one of intent: did early engineers intentionally mark out sighting points on high ground to plot routes across open country using mountains, trees and hills, dolmens, barrows and henges and, later, churches? Or are these 'mindscapes' and 'geographies of the otherworld' simply instances of modern wish fulfillment?

The first example is the St Michael Ley: a 300 mile dead-straight alignment of ancient sites stretching from St Michael's mount in Cornwall to Hopton on the east coast of England, passing through some of England's pre-eminent antiquarian sites, such as Glastonbury Tor and Avebury. The line also intersects the site of Edmund's shrine at Bury Abbey. The 'ley' follows the path of the Mayday sunrise – the Celtic festival of Beltane. Certain ley line enthusiasts are of the opinion that these alignments are in fact the 'veins of the Earth', channeling vital energy through the landscape. These energy-lines were once fertilized by ritual and celebration at certain dates in the annual calendar, specifically the solstices and equinoxes. Other proponents argue that the true nature of terrestrial currents is serpentine, not straight. In this conception, a meandering Mary Line accompanies the Michael Line, the two paths weaving in and out of one another and meeting to 'kiss' at Bury Abbey.

The second example is one of four pseudo-mythical Royal Roads of England. In the first half of the 13th century, a Benedictine monk at the Abbey of St Albans by the name of Matthew Paris drew a crude map entitled *Schema Britanniae*. Probably designed as a pilgrimage itinerary, the map plots key waymarkers along three Roman roads and one further road referred to erroneously as 'Ykenild Strete' (Icknield Street). This last road connected religious houses at Salisbury, Reading, St Albans and Bury St Edmunds. At least one researcher suggests that Matthew Paris was inspired by Geoffrey of Monmouth's *Historia Regum Britanniae*, written in roughly 1136, which describes a network of pre-Roman roads running the 'whole length of the island.' Supposedly commissioned by the legendary Celtic king Belinus, the Salisbury to Bury St Edmunds road is apparently aligned to the midsummer solstice sunrise. The king's name echoes the Celtic sun god Bel or Belenos. Confusingly, others have argued that it is in fact the St Michael Line, aligned to the Beltane sunrise, that plots the southern axis of Belinus's royal road.

It is impossible to confirm the antiquity, even the very existence, of these 'mythic pathways'. But the questing reader may wish to consider the location and significance of Bury St Edmunds in these contexts, as a hub of many pathways. One might speculate on interpretations of its earlier names, describing Bury as a 'fortunate place', or on Sigeberht's reasons for establishing his monastery there. Could the Fathers of the East Anglian church, hailing from the Celtic Christian tradition, have advised him on a propitious location? Was he following the Anglo-Saxon practice of recycling prehistoric monuments and places of ancient sanctity? A further interesting point of note is the apparent reference by Viking settlers to the area around Bury as 'The Summer Lands.' Once again, Bury and St Edmund are linked to Arthurian myth: according to the 12th century 'The Life of Gildas' by Caradoc of Llangarfan, King Melvas or Melwas was lord of the Summer Country or Summer Lands - otherwise known as Glastonbury. He abducted Queen Gwenhwyfar (Guinevere) and Arthur laid siege to Melwas's fortress, possibly on Glastonbury Tor (a site, like Bury St Edmunds, located on the St Michael Line.) Use of the term 'Summer Lands' to describe Bury perhaps chimes with the toponymy of its earlier names denoting a 'fortunate' or 'happy' place.

In summary then, the link between Edmund's kingly qualities and the land itself is made explicit in both the area's landscape features, and language itself. The sacred geometry of Bury, oriented around Edmund's shrine, is extended beyond the town: the Liberty of St Edmund and St Edmund's Ways are expressions in the landscape of the sacral king's persistent authority. The dead-straight alignments such as St Edmund's Dyke and The King's Road reinforce his moral rectitude. Meanwhile, the status of Edmund's resting-place at Bury as a place of pre-Saxon significance (and possible sanctity) is given credence by the orientation of the Fornham Cursus, the route of a Roman road connecting the Neolithic Icknield Way and Peddars Way, and the ancient King's Road. The Puddingstone Track, if it is indeed a trackway, likely includes local spurs running into Bury. Meanwhile, the 'visionary alignments' that intersect Bury, if nothing else, attest to the town's high status in England's spiritual mythology.

SELIG SUFFOLK

The eastern-most part of Britain that Edmund was born into, and inherited, has a unique quality. An understanding of this strange and ancient kingdom and its distant, otherworldly atmosphere is critical to the story of Edmund. There is something about the folk that connects them to the land yet disconnects them from the rest of the world. This sense of dislocation is written into East Anglia's history, into its very geology. After the last Ice Age, the region was joined to mainland Europe by a land bridge, known to us as Doggerland. Today, to the north, lie the lake and river systems of the Broads; to the west, the low-lying stark marshland of the Fens, now drained; to the south scuds the wide River Stour. Before drainage of the Fens began in the 17th century, the Stour would have perhaps reached to the Fenland marshes, rendering East Anglia a near-island.

The Saxon settlers, Edmund's kin, who did so much to shape the place names, patterns of settlement and culture of the region, at first looked to the east, to Sweden and Scandinavia, for their own religious and cultural cues. As we have seen, when Christianity was well established in the rest of England the East Anglian population clung to the old ways until their kings were converted. At that time, Suffolk was known as 'selig Suffolk'; 'selig' means fortunate, blessed or holy.

Even now, in the twenty-first century, large pockets of East Anglia still retain a quiet but brooding nature. 'Selig Suffolk' can still be sensed in the pull of its hedgerows, meadows and Hundred Lanes. There is a talismanic quality to the cornfields, farms and flint-towered churches, a powerful spirit of place that connects the present to its unique past:

[There is a] strange inexplicable quality... a subtle magic... It's there on the air sometimes, in certain qualities of light, at different times of the day and the year, as you walk along a lane, by a river, a lone tree or a church. It goes through you like a strange shiver, oddly chilling at times. And it's also in certain people, who are part of this quality, this energy and this place...'

The golden threads of ancient tradition, as indicated by Edmund's myth, still persist and, some say, have evolved into an esoteric tradition unique to the region. One example of this continuity is the East Anglian naming of the sun. In contrast to classical myth, Old Saxon sources depict the sun and moon as goddess and god respectively. This is continued in the East Anglian reference to the sun as 'Old Phoebe', a term used by locals until just a few generations ago.

The three crowns, the sigil of East Anglia, are part of the region's mystery. What they represent is open to interpretation. They may simply indicate the three counties composing East Anglia: Norfolk, Suffolk and Essex; they could refer to the qualities of King Edmund: his kingship, his martyrdom and his virginity. Alternatively they may allude to the three royal lines of East Anglia - the Wolsungas, Wulfingas and Heardingas. Or they could illustrate the three legendary crowns of East Anglia, buried across the region to protect it from invasion, as recounted by M. R. James in his short ghost story 'A Warning to the Curious'. Published in 1925, the tale tells of how one crown, according to the folklore, was melted down after it was found in a treasure hoard at Rendlesham. The second had been lost following the collapse of Dunwich into the sea by coastal erosion. The third crown, the last remaining defence, is still buried along the coast near Aldeburgh. It's an intriguing tale, and one that contributes to the East Anglian mythology. But until any evidence of the crowns is found we must assume the story was almost certainly concocted by the author.

Yet M. R. James's tale encapsulates the otherness of East Anglia: geographically distant, psychologically separate. Once, almost an island, protected by great ditches and legendary amulets. Even today, there is a feeling of withdrawal here. The land leans away from the rest of Britain, reaching out towards the eastern motherlands it was once joined to.

It was within this East Anglian fastness that the town eventually to become Bury St Edmunds was established. It is the region where Edmund lived, ruled, died and became England's patron saint. At Bury, his shrine was a beacon for both East Anglia and the country as a whole. And the huge popularity of his cult can be attributed to the fact that Edmund's story is a local echo of a profound cycle of myth.

The relationship between St Edmund, the town of Bury and the surrounding area illustrates in microcosm a fundamental mythic truth: the king and the land are one. Following his death, Edmund's narrative commenced a long and convoluted myth-making process. Initially, folk tales emerging from his people shaped the qualities of their dead king on the basis of their immediate needs: prosperity for the community, and protection from their enemies. Edmund's story reflected Celtic, Anglo-Saxon and Norse concepts of kingship, including notions of the king as a source of luck, peace and plenty, and a conduit for divine power. Such ideas were derived from centuries of cross-cultural pollination. A king's embodiment of these qualities was established in Anglo-Saxon royal genealogies, showing descent from corn and solar deities, Woden and Christ. One of Woden's aspects was a corn god, or barley wolf. The links between Edmund, the slain king, the corn god myth, the Wuffinga royal dynasty and Woden are all bound up in the story of Edmund's martyrdom.

While Edmund's death was later recognized as an act of Christian sacrifice, aspects of the cult of sacred kingship provided an ideological vehicle, in response to the pressing needs of the people. Firstly, Edmund's sacrifice made his authority over the land explicit; it conferred a spiritual bond that the Danish could not break. Secondly, it linked the king's death with the land's fertility; Edmund's life-force and *mana* entered the earth and nourished it. Thirdly, by embodying this tradition, Edmund's cult grew rapidly amongst Danes and Anglo-Saxons. Patterns of myth incorporating Woden, Odin, Balder and Christ were recognizable within Edmund's own narrative, and so he satisfied the needs of pagan and Christian alike.

Later, Abbo's idealized portrait of Edmund accentuated his holy and heroic aspects. The myth-making process continued at Bury St Edmunds, where Edmund's shrine was established as a sacred precinct or *temenos* from which the hero's wellspring of life-force flowed. The abbey and town were constructed around this symbolic centre, conforming to a mythic conception of a town or city and in accordance with classical traditions. Ultimately, the myth-making process fashioned a new type of saint. Edmund became a divine warrior-king, a perfect and much-loved sacred ruler who, through sacrifice, became more powerful in death than in life.

His cult achieved further rapid ascendancy as a result of Alfred's declaration of Edmund as England's first patron saint. But two other factors played a role. Firstly, his miracles, which became renowned throughout Britain and beyond, chiefly represented miracles of fertility and protection or justice. Both continued the tradition of sacred kingship, rooted in righteous judgment. These were accompanied by customs such as the Oblation of the Bull, bearing a clear pagan origin. Secondly, the link between Edmund, Bury town and his kingdom at large established the region as uniquely sacred; as 'selig Suffolk'. This relationship, forged in language and connecting kingship with moral rectitude, straightness and landscape features, confirmed Edmund's ongoing influence. His name was embedded across the kingdom in places such as the long, straight earthwork once known as St Edmund's Dyke – which demarcated a boundary of the Kingdom of East Anglia; St Edmund's Ways, and the Liberty of St Edmund itself. The town of Bury, laid out in a symbolic manner and according to ancient principles, located St Edmund's shrine such that it was an actual and spiritual focal-point. Pilgrims travelled from across Europe to see it and royalty humbled themselves before it.

The kingdom of East Anglia, Bury town and St Edmund's shrine all contributed to an archetypal vision of the sacrificed divine hero-king. The myth satisfied expectations of sacred kingship and established St Edmund's shrine as a focus of supernatural power, a place of miracles from which the king's life-force and good fortune flowed, for the

ongoing benefit of both East Anglia and the entire kingdom of England.

Edmund has frequently been re-interpreted and re-invented for all manner of politico-religious and propagandist ends. His banner, for instance, was a powerful relic, and symbolic of the saint's potency. It was borne by the victors at the battle of Fornham in 1173 and taken into the battle of Agincourt in 1415. The new interpretation outlined in these pages paints Edmund as a figure with mythic resonance, and as a product of many traditions of belief. In that sense he has become inclusive and non-denominational. The exploration of this wider context reveals Edmund as a profoundly significant mythic figure; a divine king, a sentinel, a national hero. Hopefully this interpretation will go some way towards ensuring Edmund's full rehabilitation in the hearts and minds of the nation.

NOTES AND REFERENCES

Introduction

"2,000 coins were minted in his memory...": Klaniczay pg 89
"An indication of where Vikings settled...": Palmer (2002) pg 110
"His cult spread as far north as Scandinavia and Iceland": see Bale ch 2: 'Chronology, Genealogy and Conversion: The Afterlife of St Edmund in the North' by Alison Finlay
"Certainly its most popular pilgrimage destination": Bale pg 4
"A centre of artistic splendour and culture...": Dymond and Northeast pg 36

Glory and Shield of the East Angles

"...son of Æthelweard or Ealhhere...": see Hervey, Preface 43
"...Some tales tell of Edmund's brother...": Ibid, Preface 41
"By 597 the majority of Anglo-Saxon kingdoms...": Yorke pg 2-4
"Suffolk's 500 parish names are spelled very much as they are now": Scarfe (1986) pg 13
"They were ultimately responsible for establishing the Kingdom...": Whittock pg 164
"...one thirteenth of the total population of Britain": Green pg 125
"...a standard and scepter, clothing and even a pillow": Carver (1998) pg 128
"...some recent DNA studies have shown": for a general introduction to this complex, fascinating and fast-changing area see Shaw. For a more detailed presentation of the research, see Weale, Weiss, Jager, Bradman and Thomas.
"...Celts probably continued to live in East Anglia...": Enright pg 76
"...raiding churches and communities around Huntington": See Gray
"The most credible theory..": See Hervey, Preface 43
The subsequent account of St Edmund's life and death is a distillation of the efforts of others. I have drawn liberally from Hervey, Winterbottom, Crossley-Holland and Mackinlay
"Edmund was, in every sense, an ideal ruler": Klaniczay pg 91
"...miserably destroyed God's church... by rapine and slaughter": Harrison pg 10
"Little more was heard of the Vikings until 835": Ibid pg 40
"The number of ships increases...": Oliver pg 147
"King Æthelred and his son Alfred...": See Ferguson, ch4
"...wedding parties would avoid it": See the 'Hoxne' entry at hiddenea.com
"...or Hellesdon near Norwich": See Mason
"Edmund's holy cousin, St Fremund...": Fornasini pg 37
"Both sites are roughly five miles from Bury": Meeres pg 12
"Archaeological evidence shows that both rivers were settled...": Dymond and Martin pg 37
"He was entirely fresh as if he were alive": Crossley-Holland pg 231
"...one of whom was named Oswen": Klaniczay pg 91

"Cnut offered the saint a votive gold crown from his own head": Carlyle pg 46
"Edward usually walking the last mile...": Adair pg 104
"Edmund rapidly gained status as a protector": Ridyard pg 226-30
"In another document": Namely Samsonis Abbatis Opus De Miraculis Sancti Aedmundi
"This roll call clearly emphasizes Edmund's healing power": Fornasini pg 39-40
"...so that the holy places should be more carefully and diligently kept": Jocelin of Brakelond pg 171-7
"Edmund's body is buried beneath tennis courts": See Ghaemi
"...simply that he was killed by the Danes": Bale pg 2
"...non-violence as the proper path of a holy king": Damon pg 177, 182
"Abbo adapted these standard motifs as he saw fit": See Gransden for example, pg 87
"...it is reasonable to assume that oral culture...": Salih pg 36

The Slain King

"Abbo introduced the notion that death was Edmund's ultimate duty": Damon pg 184
"A retainer without a lord was essentially an outcast": Crossley-Holland pg 46-7
'The Wanderer' quotation: Ibid pg 51-2
"...he became holy in both life and death": Damon pg 172
"O St Edmund the King!": Klaniczay pg 89
"An indication of where Vikings settled...": Palmer (2002) pg 110
"the Danes paid lip-service to Edmund's cult...": Bale pg 2
"...they were separated by cultural and religious boundaries...": Thomas (2003) pg 28
"...there is little evidence of their impact on place names...": Rye pg 6-7. The few Danish names in Suffolk include: Snape, Lowestoft, Lound, Ashby, Barnby and Risby.
"...the primary allegiance of an individual was no longer to a family...": Carver (1998) pg 104
"...kinship, moral values and heroic reputations...": Crossley-Holland pg x
"...the mystery of life-in-death...": Frazer pg 264-66, Grimassi pg 84-6
"...preserve the regenerative spirit that flowed through their regent": Frazer pg 265-8
"...an altar where carrion was picked clean...": See Pryor (2008) ch 13
"...traversed in shamanic activities to obtain knowledge and wisdom": Greenwood pg 82
"he represented procreative power, the seed of life": Grimassi pg 84-6
"he fertilized the earth and ensured his people a good harvest": Pinch pg 178-9, Frazer pg 362-72
Quote by the The National Museum of Ireland's Head of Antiquities: See TheJournal.ie: 'Bog Body Found in Co Laois Could Be That of Sacrificed King'
"...a king's personal qualities were linked to the general wellbeing of the land": Spence (1971) pg 134
"In 1984 a peat body was found in Britain...": See Ross and Robins
For more on the possible Celtic origins of the Sutton Hoo sceptre and its meaning and symbolism in relation to sacred kingship, see Enright
"...the king is described as being hung to the corn mother...": Grigsby pg 127-8

Ynglinga Saga quote: Somerville and McDonald pg 100
"The Ynglings dynasty traced their descent from Frey...": Frazer pg 179, Chaney pg 94
"Oswald of Northumbria's body...": Chaney pg 96
"Haelu was suffused throughout the cosmos...": Bates pg 114
"It was also believed that life force lingered after death...": Trubshaw pg 41-2
"...become a charismatic embodiment of that magical force": Chaney pg 12, 15
"Beaw, Sceldwa and Sceaf were personifications of that same process": Herbert pg 15-16
"...according to the tale of John Barleycorn...": See Grigsby ch 16
"...was considered a lucky day for sowing and planting crops": Chaney pg 35
"...recall 'the ancient cult-war and the heroic deeds of Edmund's ancestors'...": Grigsby pg 204-5
"...ritual sacrifice amongst pagan German traditions...": Chaney pg 187
"...certainly prevalent amongst Viking raiders": see Smyth for a more thorough overview of Viking human sacrifice in Britain and Ireland
"Another suggestion is the bodies were of ideological 'deviants'...": Carver (1998) pg 137-43
"...there is very little evidence to distinguish one from another": Reynolds pg 52
"...a god who, by self-sacrifice, won knowledge for the benefit of man": Branston pg 97
"The other gods made sport...": Ibid pg 168
"...the Danes threw spears and shot arrows at Edmund...": Adair pg 104
"...but new growth would sprout from the head of the dead plant...": Grigsby pg 178
"The bearer of the name was an emblematic figure...": Newton pg 106
"If there was a fundamental shift, it was in the Romano-Celts themselves...": Carver (1992) pg 14
"...wolves frequently figure in the role of helpful animals": Ross pg 341-2
"...in much the same way as Odin's valkyries": Branston pg 107
"Continuity existed in Celtic, Saxon and other cultures...": Warner pg 77
"Woden / Odin has his origins in Celtic myth": Grigsby pg 49
"There are certainly parallels between Thor and Odin...": Ross and Robins pg 47
"Celtic human sacrifice included shooting victims...": Pennick (1997) pg 76
"Irish tales tell of King Cormac...": Enright pg 53-4
Examples of Celtic veneration for the head in lives of Celtic Christian saints: Ross pg 108-9
"The ill and infirm journeyed there...": hiddenea.com: http://bit.ly/14Nv31r
"Celtic-style stone heads have been found built into Danish churches": Ross and Robins pg 161
"One interpretation of the Green Knight's complex and contradictory nature...": Besserman pg 220
"...depictions of the sun are accompanied by stalks of grain...": Lilly pg 10
"...cannot answer these mystical questions and remains at the Grail Castle": Spence (1993) pg 167
"The mystery at the heart of the grail is service...": Matthews pg 93
"...when Britain shall require his aid once more": Spence (1993) pg 154
"...the dead king who continues to be powerful, even in death": Frankfort pg 207

"Parts of his corpse ended up at Bury abbey": Hoggett pg 49
"...was later denounced as a 'god of the field'...": Parish pg 88 (1997) pg 20-1

Herb, Rood and Remedy

"The dualism that exists today between Christianity and 'paganism'...": see Trubshaw (2013) pg 14-16
"...regarded as a local incarnation of the Roman solar god Apollo": Pennick (1997) pg 70
"It was a custom of the pagans...": Hutton (2001) pg 1
Quotation from letter to Abbot Mellitus: Bates pg 53
"In his personal temple was set up one altar to Christ...": Wilson pg 34
"every village seemed to have its own saint and holy place": Palmer (2002) pg 103
"Christianity arrived in Britain with the Romans...": Ibid pg 60
"Likely to have been well established in Britain by 600BC...": Ross and Robins pg 130, although Hutton puts the date closer to 200BC
"...a solar deity and dispenser of light and healing": Pennick (1997) pg 72
"This powerful and active cult was found throughout the Celtic world": Ross pg 61-2, 124-6
"...originating in the Iron Age but continuing into Roman occupation": Watts pg 136
"...the church began to crumble and the old beliefs took hold once more": See Watts, ch 3
"...rooted in the earlier traditions of nature, learning and locality...": Palmer (2002) pg 78
"...sinful as argued in Roman dogma": Ibid pg 65
"Druids took on the mantle of priests...": Bradley pg viii
"...reinforced the image of nature-lovers...": Bradley pg 3, 10, 11, 21
"...a harvest celebration occurred near Eton...": Herbert pg 19
"The range of harvest celebrations...": Hutton (1996) pg 341-2
"May rites, practised after seed time in rural cultures...": Bucknell pg 186
"... at least four of the Æsir gods were venerated...": Branston pg 41
"...they reworked prehistoric monuments into the fabric of their culture": Semple (2013), Preface
"...worship seems to have taken place in open-air sanctuaries...": See Semple
"...use of hills and open spaces was a expression of ongoing Romano-Celtic beliefs": Heslop: 'Paganism in Early Anglo-Saxon East Anglia' by Tim Pestell, pg 72, 75
"...the objects may well have been employed as talismans": Ibid pg 80-4
"Belief began dying out by the eighth century...": North pg 80
"...their hounds were pitch black with staring hideous eyes": Ibid pg 94
"Thor the god of serfs and the working class...": Chaney pg 34
"...over 10,000 English were baptized...": Cusack pg 98
"He was baptized in Kent...": North pg 321
"...the House of Wessex was extended beyond Woden...": Ibid pg 112
"...Woden destroyed an evil force with Christ's gift of herbs": Ibid pg 85-8
"There are further parallels with the Norse god Balder": Branston pg 168
"pagan songs and poems were even favoured by monks": See Wood: Beowulf

"Felix was ordained by the Archbishop of Canterbury...": Hoggett pg 50

"...endowed land at Cnobheresburg...": Dymond and Northeast, pg 27

"perhaps this explains Felix's omission": Bradley pg viii

"...Sigeberht was tolerant of the both the Roman and Celtic traditions...": Scarfe (1986) pg 47

"...minster churches enabled the religion to reach out...": Heslop: 'Paganism in Early Anglo-Saxon East Anglia' by Tim Pestell, pg 71

"...the risk of failed harvests or division from their ancestors in the afterlife...": Berend pg 19

"He formally renounced his empty superstitions...": Wilson pg 30

"The act of spear-throwing may have echoed the behaviour of Germanic pagans...": Ibid pg 31

Changing burial rites in Norfolk and Suffolk: Hogget pg 81, 114, 116

"...a Bronze Age palisade and Neolithic ditch have been discovered...": Carver pg 107

"...previously cemeteries were located at the periphery": Higham and Ryan, pg 206

"...to explicitly establish a link between the Wuffingas...": Newton pg 135

"...the church suffered, and its organization was shattered": Hadley (2006) pg 193

"Further destruction may have been suffered...": See The St Edmundsbury Chronicle: http://bit.ly/11c66NA

"...and monastic life revived at Bury": Dymond and Northeast pg 31

"places of execution would have been an everyday sight...": Reynolds pg 1

"The Danes were *halbgloubig*...": Lynch pg 72-4

"The laws of Cnut expressly forbade...": Branston pg 54

"It also appears in the epic tale of Beowulf": Ibid pg 65

"The Old English Maxims...": Cavill pg 133

"...a magical remedy for protection against elves and goblins is provided": Crossley-Holland pg 276

"Hail to you, Earth, Mother of Mortals...": Herbert pg 15

Description of the Oblation of the Bull: Gilligwater, pg 142-9

"The Druidic culture-god Hu...": Spence (1970) pg 177

"They were magical animals...": Ross pg 307

"...small herds of white cattle were preserved...": Spence (1993) pg 45

"...saints played a key role in this...": Bremmer pg 118

"...a physical, localized expression of Christian virtues": Watkins pg 121

"...on account of a relic from the shrine of St Edmund...": Ibid pg 123

Villa Regia, Axis Mundi

The hero's relationship to the physical centre of the myth: Campbell pg 35

"...the burial place of a king was extremely holy": Chaney pg 94

"Some observers have suggested that Edmund's early veneration...": see Mason, 'St Edmund and the Vikings' ch 7

"Bury's strategic importance ...": Hoggett pg 2

Summary of archaeological finds close to Bury: See Birch

Fornham cursus: Authors and researchers Nigel Pennick and Paul Devereux surveyed a large number of cursus in the later 80s, and their findings are summarized here.

Summary of cursus features: Pennick and Devereux pg 48-51

"...there are a number of other possible cursus in the region...": At Pakenham, Flempton, Long Melford, Bottisham and Stratford St Mary. See http://bit.ly/13XpNfT

"Theories of their purpose include processional or ritual paths...": Devereux (2003) pg 69-72

"With its axis extended it would pass through, or very near to, the abbey precinct": Pennick and Devereux pg 61-2

'...thought to denote a hill of observation, from the Old English totian...": See http://bit.ly/Zuhh2k

"...finds have been located in many villages surrounding Bury...": Including Risby, Little and Great Whelnetham, Stanningfield, Rougham, Pakenham, Hengrave and Ixworth.

"The village may have been a Roman station...": See Birch

"...the commander of the 14th Legion had his Praetorium...": Yates pg 2-3

"A Roman votive figurine, depicting the god Mars, was found in the town": Warner pg 55

"...four carved stone heads were unearthed...": Deck pg 4

"...a proposed Roman road linking the Icknield Way...": See Birch

"'bederic' signifies prosperous, happy and pleasant...": Yates pg 6

"They made no vows and were free to marry...": Meeres pg 13

"A new church, probably a round wooden structure...": Deck pg 36

"The octagonal base of the Virgin's Cross survives today": Meeres pg 14

"In 1020 he commanded thirteen monks from St Bene's to colonise Bury": See http://bit.ly/UzUUbF

"the entire land endowment was referred to as the 'Liberty of St Edmund'": Meeres pg 15

"At this time, the town's market was located at the junction of Westgate St": Ibid pg 4-5

"As the abbey grew, so did the town...": Beckley pg 74, Scarfe pg 5

"Bury's defences were a mix of wall, river and earthwork...": Beckley pg 74-5

"Baldwin organized the reconstruction of the abbey church...": Pennick and Devereux pg 131

"...conceiving a plan according to symbolic principles": Ibid pg 131, 97

"...suggests continuity from before the founding of the abbey": Ibid pg 95

"The symbolic nature of Bury's layout was not restricted to the abbey...": Murdie pg 9

"...using stone from as far away as Caen": Deck pg 39

"At its height, Bury abbey contained...": Dymond and Northeast pg 36

"...frequent contacts with the University of Oxford": Fornasini pg 36

"700 monasteries were founded in England": See English Heritage (2011) pg 5

"Bury abbey was the fourth richest": Scarfe (1997) pg 6

"The landed estates of the abbey dominated the region...": Dymond and Northeast pg 33

"No other market existed within six miles...": Bailey pg 39, 119, 128, 129

"The bones of King Anna...": Pennick pg 14

"A pardon bowl absolved anyone who drank from it...": Morris pg 121

"the 15th century chronicler William Worcester observed...": Webb pg 144
"For Celts, they were the focus of cult practice and ritual...": Ross pg 20, 105
"The shrine itself consisted of gold plates...": Nilson pg 120
"Four candles burned continuously...": Ibid pg 137

The Kingdom of East Anglia

"Kings, as conduits for divine energies...": Enright pg 87, 292
"The Indo-European root words reg...": Sullivan (2005) pg 70-2; Pennick and Devereux
pg 246-8
"Bible references also link straight paths with divine kingship and righteousness":
Sullivan (2005) pg 72
"Abbo described the Kingdom of East Anglia as 'water-girdled'": Roxby pg 161
"The area to the east was divided into the Liberty of St Etheldreda...": Scarfe (1972) pg
41-2
"The Hundreds, recorded in Domesday Book...": Ibid pg 113
"The most spectacular surviving example...": Ibid
"...it demarcated the western edge of both the Kingdom of East Anglia...": Warner pg 148
"It's function as both a physical boundary...": see Enright pg 267-9
"Thereafter, the need for a strong defensive bulwark...": Green pg 146-7
"The westerly ditches...": Williamson pg 40
"...considering construction of the entire earthwork occurred simultaneously...": Pennick
and Devereux pg 118
"The ditch marks four parish boundaries...": Ibid pg 117
"Although the defensive bank has been leveled, the ditch remains deep in place...": Ibid
pg 116-7
"The bodies faced eastwest...": Ibid pg 116
"The former terminates in a pond...": Toulson pg 149
Beowulf quotation describing Grendel: Heaney pg 9
"Beowulf was authored in East Anglia...": Newton pg 135
"Marshlands and bogs were dangerously deceptive...": Bates pg 83
"The Suffolk village of Grundisburgh...": See Dr Sam Newman's site at: http://bit.ly/
YQefo8
"These green lanes were originally used by pilgrims...": Pretty ch 12
"...The King's Road or King's Highway...": Codrington ch4
"The way is not thought to be a single track...": Macfarlane pg 41, 44
"In East Anglia the way is particularly ill-defined...": Heath and Michell pg 94
"The Icknield Way would have been used for centuries...": Bulfield pg 1-13
"...a great nation-spanning road defined by King Belinus...": Heath and Michell pg 94
"Alternatively, the Icknield Way may have been a trade and migration route...": Bulfield
pg 127
"The Way finally terminates in Wiltshire...": Ibid pg 150-1
"A network of roads was established across the entire country...": Peel pg 1

"...the road would have forked south to provide a route directly to Bury Abbey...": See Birch

Summary of the Puddingstone Trail: See The Megalithic Portal at http://www. megalithic.co.uk

"Critics argue that Rudge simply plotted a route...": See Pennick (1970), 'Thorgrim'

"The first example is the St Michael Ley...": for readers interested in this topic, the following publications are suggested: 'The New View Over Atlantis' by John Michell (1986) and 'The Sun and the Serpent' by Paul Broadhurst and Hamish Miller (1990)

"...the Salisbury to Bury St Edmunds road is apparently aligned...": see Robb pg 220 and ch 14

Selig Suffolk

"[There is a] strange inexplicable quality...": Barnes: Jill Bruce on East Anglia

"Old customs still persist...": See Pennick (1995)

"Old Saxon sources depict the sun and moon...": Branston pg 51

".... a term used by locals...": Pennick (1995) pg 69. Also, Hugh Barrett mentions in 'Early to Rise' (1967) the common use of 'Old Phoebe' or 'Bright Phoebe' by Suffolk men of his, or older, generations – see pg 137

"...we must assume the story was almost certainly concocted by the author": See James

"It was borne by the victors at the battle of Fornham...": Nilson pg 52

BIBLIOGRAPHY

Adair, John: *The Pilgrim's Way* (1978)

Anon: *A Concise Description of Bury St. Edmund's: And Its Environs, Within the Distance of Ten Miles* (1827)

Ashe, Geoffrey: *King Arthur's Avalon: The Story of Glastonbury* (9th ed) (1986)

Bailey, Mark: *Medieval Suffolk: an Economic and Social History 1200-1500* (2007)

Bailey, Michael David: *Magic And Superstition in Europe: A Concise History from Antiquity to the Present* (2006)

Bale, Anthony (ed): *St Edmund, King and Martyr: Changing Images of a Medieval Saint* (2009)

Barnes, Richard: *The Sun in the East – Norfolk and Suffolk Fairs* (1983)

Bates, Brian: *The Real Middle Earth* (2002)

Beckley, Rene: *Ancient Walls of East Anglia* (1979)

Berend, Nora: *Christianization and the Rise of Christian Monarchy* (2007)

Besserman, Lawrence: 'The Idea of the Green Man', ELH, Vol 53, No.2 (1986)

Birch, Mel: *Suffolk's Ancient Sites, Historic Places* (2004)

Black, Joseph: *The Broadview Anthology of British Literature: The Medieval Period* (2nd ed) (2009)

Blackman, Mark: 'Presidential Address: Currency Under the Vikings parts 1 & 2', British Numismatic Journal, No.76 (2006)

Bradley, Ian C: *Celtic Christianity: Making Myths and Chasing Dreams* (1999)

Branston, Brian: *The Lost Gods of England* (1974)

Bremmer, Jan N; Veenstra, Jan Riepke: *The Metamorphosis of Magic: From Late Antiquity to the Early Modern Period* (2002)

British Academy - *Royal Historical Society Joint Committee on Anglo-Saxon Charters,* Bury St Edmunds entry: http://bit.ly/UzUUbF (2011)

Bryant, Arthur: 'The Story of England: The End of the Saxon Kingdom', History Today, Vol 3 Issue 8 (1953)

Bucknell, Peter A: 'Entertainment and Ritual, 600-1600' (1979)

Bulfield, Anthony: *The Icknield Way* (1972)

Burgess, Mike: 'Hidden East Anglia': http://bit.ly/11CD50t (n.d.)

Carlyle, Thomas: *Past and Present, Chartism and Sartor Resartus* (1862)

Campbell, Joseph: *The Hero With a Thousand Faces* (1968)

Campbell, James: *The Anglo-Saxon State* (2000)

Carver, Martin: *Sutton Hoo: Burial Ground of Kings?* (1998)

Carver, Martin O.H: *The Age of Sutton Hoo: The Seventh Century in North-Western Europe* (1992)

Cavill, Paul: *Maxims in Old English Poetry* (1999)

Chaney, William A: *The Cult of Kingship in Anglo-Saxon England: The Transition from Paganism to Christianity* (1970)

Codrington, Thomas: *Roman Roads of Britain* (1903)

Cox, R. Hippisley: *The Green Roads of England* (3rd ed) (1927)

Crossley-Holland, Kevin: *The Anglo-Saxon World: An Anthology* (2009 ed)

Cusack, Carole M: *Conversion Amongst the Germanic People* (1998)

Damon, John Edward: *Soldier Saints and Holy Warriors: Warfare and Sanctity in the Literature of Early England* (2003)

Deck, J: *A Guide to the Town, Abbey and Antiquities of Bury St. Edmunds* (1923)

Devereux, Paul: *Spirit Roads* (2007)

Devereux, Paul: *Symbolic Landscapes: Dreamtime Earth and Avebury's Open Secret* (1992)

Dymond, David; Northeast, Peter: *A History of Suffolk* (1985)

Dymond, David; Martin, Edward (ed): *An Historical Atlas of Suffolk* (1988)

English Heritage: *English Heritage's Record of Scheduled Monuments: Bury St Edmunds Abbey*: http://bit.ly/TzPM7s (2011)

Enright, Michael J: *The Sutton Hoo Sceptre and the Roots of Celtic Kingship Theory* (2006)

Frankfort, Henry: *Kingship and the Gods: A Study of Ancient Near Eastern Religion as the Integration of Society and Nature* (Oriental Institute Essays) (1978)

Fraser, James: *The Golden Bough* (Wordsworth ed) (1993)

Fornasini, Ilaria: *'St Edmund of East Anglia and His Miracles Through the Centuries: Variations in Literature and Art'*, Quest Magazine no.6 (2009)

Ghaemi, Mariam: *'Bury St Edmunds: Should we launch a fresh search for St Edmund's body?'* East Anglian Daily Times (2013): http://bit.ly/164cUjE

Godfrey, John: *The Church in Anglo-Saxon England* (1962)

Gransden, Antonia: *Legends, Tradition and History in Medieval England* (1992)

Gray, Arthur: *'On the Late Survival of a Celtic Population in East Anglia'*, paper read to the Cambridge Antiquarian Society (1911)

Green, Charles: Sutton Hoo: *The Excavation of a Royal Ship-Burial* (1963)

Greenaway, Diana; Sayers, Jane: *Chronicle of the Abbey of Bury St. Edmunds by Jocelin of Brakelond* (World Classics ed) (1989)

Greenwood, Susan: *The Nature of Magic: An Anthropology of Consciousness* (2005)

Grigsby, John: *Beowulf & Grendel: The Truth Behind England's Oldest Legend* (2005)

Grimassi, Raven: *Crafting Wiccan Traditions* (2008)

Hall, Martina (dir): *Face of Britain* (2008)

Heaney, Seamus (trans): *Beowulf: An Illustrated Edition* (2008)

Herbert, Kathleen: *Looking For The Lost Gods of England* (1994)

Hervey, Lord Francis: *Corolla Sancti Eadmundi* (1907)

Heslop, T.A; Mellings, Elizabeth; Thofner, Margit: *Art, Faith and Place in East Anglia: From Prehistory to Present* (2012)

Higham, Nicholas J; Ryan, Martin J: *The Landscape Archaeology of Anglo-Saxon England* (2010)

Hoggett, Richard: *The Archaeology of the East Anglian Conversion* (2010)

Hooke, Della: *Trees in Anglo-Saxon England: Literature, Lore and Landscape* (2010)

Hope-Taylor, Brian: *Yeavering: an Anglo-British Centre of Early Northumbria* (1977)

Hugn, William (Trans): *The Life of Gildas by a Monk of Rhys and Caradoc of Llancarfan* (2000)

Hutton, Ronald: *Blood and Mistletoe: The History of the Druids in Britain* (2009)

Hutton, Ronald: *The Stations of the Sun: A History of the Ritual Year in Britain* (2001)

James, M R: *A Warning to the Curious and Other Stories* (1998 ed)

Klaniczay, Gábor: *Holy Rulers and Blessed Princesses: Dynastic Cults in Medieval Central Europe* (2002)

Koch, John T: *Celtic Culture: A Historical Encyclopedia* (2006)

Lynch, Joseph H: *Christianizing Kinship: Ritual Sponsorship in Anglo-Saxon England* (1998)

Macfarlane, Robert: *The Old Ways: A Journey on Foot* (2012)

Mackinlay, Rev. J. B: *Saint Edmund, King and Martyr. A History of His Life and Times, with an Account of the Translations of His Incorrupt Body* (1893)

Mason, Joseph: *Edmund of East Anglia* (n.d.)

Mason, Joseph: *St Edmund and the Vikings 869-1066* (n.d.)

Meeres, Frank: *A History of Bury St Edmunds* (2002)

Morris, Colin; Roberts, Peter: *Pilgrimage: The English Experience from Becket to Bunyan* (2002)

Murdie, Alan: *Haunted Bury St Edmunds* (2006)

Newton, Sam: *The Origins of Beowulf and the Pre-Viking Kingdom of East Anglia* (1993)

Nilson, Ben: *Cathedral Shrines of Medieval England* (1998)

North, Richard: *Heathen Gods in Old English Literature* (1997)

Oliver, Neil: *Vikings* (2012)

Palmer, Martin: *The Sacred History of Britain* (2002)

Parish, Helen L: *Monks, Miracles and Magic: Reformation Representations of the Medieval Church* (2005)

Peel, J.H.B: *Along the Roman Roads of Britain* (1971)

Pennick, Nigel: *The Sacred World of The Celts* (1997)

Pennick, Nigel: *Secrets of East Anglian Magic* (1995)

Pennick, Nigel; Devereux, Paul: *Lines on the Landscape: Leys and Other Linear Enigmas* (1989)

Pennick, Nigel: 'The Puddingstone Track', Lantern Magazine no.13 (1970)

Pinch, Geraldine: *Egyptian Mythology: A Guide to the Gods, Goddesses, and Traditions of Ancient Egypt* (2002)

Powlesland, Dominic: *The Heslerton Parish Project: 20 years of archaeological research in the Vale of Pickering* (2000)

Reynolds, Andrew: *Anglo-Saxon Deviant Burial Customs* (2009)

Ridyard, Susan J: *The Royal Saints of Anglo-Saxon England: A Study of West Saxon and East Anglian Cults* (1988)

Robb, Graham: *The Ancient Paths* (2013)

Ross, Anne: *Pagan Celtic Britain: Studies in Iconography and Tradition* (1996)

Ross, Anne; Robins, Don: *The Life and Death of a Druid Prince* (1989)

Roxby, Percy M: *East Anglia* (1902)

Rye, James: *A Popular Guide to Suffolk Place Names* (1997)

Salih, Sarah (ed): *A Companion to Middle English Hagiography* (2006)

Scarfe, Norman: Jocelin of Brakelond: *The Life of a Monk and Chronicler of the Great Abbey of Bury St Edmunds* (1997)

Scarfe, Norman: *The Suffolk Landscape* (1972)
Scarfe, Norman: *Suffolk in the Middle Ages* (1986)
Semple, Sarah: *'Defining the OE Hearg: A preliminary archaeological and topographic examination of hearg place names and their hinterlands'* Early Medieval Europe (2007)
Semple, Sarah: *Perceptions of the Prehistoric in Anglo-Saxon England: Religion, Ritual and Rulership in the Landscape* (2013)
Shaw, Jonathan: *'Who Killed the Men of England?'*, Harvard Magazine (2009)
Smyth, Alfred P: *Scandinavian Kings in the British Isles, 850-880* (1977)
Somerville, Angus A; McDonald, Russell Andrew: *The Viking Age: A Reader* (2010)
Spence, Lewis: *The Mysteries of Britain: Secret Rites and Traditions of Ancient Britain* (Antiquarian Press ed) (1970)
Spence, Lewis: *The Mysteries of Celtic Britain* (1905)
Spence, Lewis: *The Magic Arts in Celtic Britain* (Dorset House ed) (1993)
Spence, Lewis: *The History and Origins of Druidism* (1971 ed)
Statham, Margaret: *The Book of Bury St Edmunds* (1997)
Sweet, Henry; Cutler, Kenneth (trans*): Anglo-Saxon Primer* (1961)
Taylor, Christopher: *Roads and Tracks of Britain* (1979)
TheJournal.ie: *'Bog Body Found in Co Laois Could Be That of Sacrificed King'*: http://bit.ly/qYV80l (2011)
'Thorgrim': *'The Puddingstone Trail – Fact or Fantasy?'* The Megalithic Portal: http://bit.ly/10lDC74
Toulson, Shirley: *East Anglia: Walking the Ley Lines and Ancient Tracks* (1981)
Trubshaw, Bob: *Souls, Spirits and Deities* (2012)
Trubshaw, Bob: *Continuity of Worldviews in Anglo-Saxon England* (2013)
Tymms, Samuel: *A handbook of Bury St Edmunds, with additions by J. R. Thompson* (1885)
Warner, Peter M: *The Origins of Suffolk* (1996)
Watkins, C.S: *History and the Supernatural in Medieval England* (2007)
Watts, Dorothy: *Religion in Late Roman Britain: Forces of Change* (2002)
Weale, Michael E; Weiss, Deborah A; Jager, Rolf F; Bradman, Neil; Thomas, Mark G: *'Y Chromosome Evidence for Anglo-Saxon Mass Migration'*, Oxford Journal of Molecular Biology and Evolution, Volume 19 Issue 7 (2002)
Webb, Diana: *Pilgrimage in Medieval England* (2000)
Whitelock, Dorothy (ed): *'Fact and Fiction in the Legend of St Edmund'*, Proceedings of the Suffolk Institute of Archaeology XXXI (1970)
Whittock, Martyn J: *The Origins of England 410-600* (1986)
Williams, Howard: *Death and Memory in Early Medieval Britain* (2006)
Williamson, Tom: *The Origins of Hertfordshire* (2010)
Wilson, David: *Anglo-Saxon Paganism* (1992)
Winterbottom, Michael: *Three Lives of English Saints* (1972)
Wood, Michael: *Beowulf* (2009)
Yates, Richard: *An Illustration of the Monastic History and Antiquities of the Town and Abbey of St Edmund's Bury* (1805)
Yorke, Barbara: *Kings and Kingdoms of Early Anglo-Saxon England* (2003)

APPENDIX

A short selection of poems, new and old, on the subject of St Edmund.

The Psalm of St Edmund

In the form of an acrostic of his name

Sing praises to the Lord, O you His Saints, *Psalm 30.4*
Take thy seat on high. *7.7*

Earth is satisfied with the fruit of thy work. *104.13*
Deeds of the Lord, His wondrous works; *107.24*
Magnify the Lord with me. *34.3*
Understand this: *73.16*
Now my head shall be lifted up above my enemies, *27.6*
Dwelling in the House of the Lord for ever. *23.6*

The Rt Revd Charles Mugleston

The King and the Land

I will tell of Edmund, great king of the East Angles;
His deeds, devotion and cunning are well known.
Born of one hanging lord but loyal to another,
His people honoured their king in both ways, according to their beliefs.
I knew this man and the paths he trod in those days of renown.

When the king first came here, he kissed me, and I loved him.
They were fortunate times, and none could recall their like.
The barley ripened and drooped,
And Edmund honoured his lords and kinsmen from the gift-throne.
I too knew delight in those days of good cheer.

Then came war-smiths from across the whale-lanes.
The Danish horde shook their glistening ash-spears.
Edmund's mead-hall emptied,
And the proud king and his warriors awaited their enemy.
I heard their battle-song as they fed the blood-field.

Fate lay waste to Edmund's brave earls;
His hearth-companions lay dead amongst the crows.
Those boastful Danes bound the king,
And made slow slaughter of him under the oaken hearg.
I wept for gentle Edmund in the darkening day.

This was the wyrd of the god-sprung wolf-king.
But even as his kinsmen covered him with dark clods,
The ear that was struck from the sheaf stirred again.
O Edmund, king-in-the-ground who breathes blessings,
I embraced you then, and still do, and we are one.

This is the mystery of Edmund the slaughtered god-king:
wolf-kin, martyr, glory of East Anglia and protector of all England.

Mark Taylor

The Fall of Edmund, King of the East Angles

A Traditionary Tale

The morn arose and shot her ray,
Resplendent, from the clime of day,
Along the wide extended heath,
Which night beheld a scene of death.
The tents of England's King gleam'd white,
Reflected from the dawning light.
Fast o'er the misty hills, afar,
The Chief of Lochlin urg'd the car,
And wak'd to strife th' adventurous war:
His standards, streaming to the sky,
Led forth his troops to victory.
With eagle glance, the Monarch stood
And view'd the fatal field of blood,
Then urg'd his valiant few to stand,
The guardians of their native land;
The spirits of the mighty dead
Leaned from the Heavens, o'er Conflict's bed,
Intent to hear th' expiring sigh,
The dying moan of Liberty.
Inguar approached, Death in his rear,
And on his van, Revenge and Fear.
Each line advanced – the battle woke,
And reddened at each echoing stroke;
Sword rang on helm, and spear on shield;
Each chieftan doubtful held the field –
Oppression swayed the Danish heart,
But Freedom nerved the English dart.
Long raged the thick fight's furious bray;
With blood bedewed – a fallen prey –
Lay high-piled ranks of countless dead,
The Heavens their shroud – the heath their bed –
The bannered Raven, tow'ring, waved
O'er Edmund's ranks. In vain they braved
The ruthless fury of their foe,

For Victory sat on Inguar's brow.
Distraction seized on Edmund's soul,
And o'er his senses phrenzy stole.

The day's declining ray was past,
And evening's mist the sky o'ercast,
Uncertain of the trackless space,
The vanquish'd Monarch urg'd his pace,
Till Eglesdene's high rising fane,
At distance, cheer'd the gloomy plain;
With weeds o'ergrown, an ancient pile
Of mossy bricks, and Runic style.
The Waveny's sedgy confines bore
A passage safe from either shore.
Urged by mistrust, the Monarch sped,
And gladly sought its friendly shade;
Securely, there he silent lay,
Till Luna rose, with burnish'd ray,
And through the regions of the West
Raised high in air her silver crest.

From Hymen's rite, a youthful pair
Were speeding, by the evening star –
They passed the bridge; the moon's soft beam
Fell radiant on the ripling stream,
And to the wanderers on the shore
Betrayed the spurs that Edmund wore:
Suspicion seized each wondering mind,
And, faster than the rising wind,
They hastened to the long-past gate,
Eager to point their King's retreat.

Ill-fated Monarch! Once the dread
Of foreign foes – thy hopes are fled!
How chang'd thy fate! The rising day
Beheld thee England's sceptre sway;
It's dying beams illume the breast
Of Edmund – now pale Sorrow's guest:
A suppliant at a conquerer's throne,
E'en on the shores so late his own.

Submissive at a victor's frown,
Usurper of thy country's crown;
Chain'd to the stake – by anguish torn,

Thy hurried breast must know the scorn
Of murd'rers, happy in thy moan;
Thy fortune lost, thy honours flown.
Not sorrow, torture, pangs unsung
Can wrench confession from his tongue,
But, glorying in his noble death,
He, calm, resigns his parting breath.

But hark – the dying martyr speaks,
From his parch'd lips his last will breaks:
"Cursed be the spot where Edmund lay –
Dimm'd in that spot be Luna's ray –
May execrations tend the pair,
Who o'er the fatal arch repair
From Hymen's sainted altars free;
May hate – unknown mortality –
Attend their lives; domestic strife,
And all the ills of wedded life;
May anguish seal their dying breath –
And fell remorse – woe worse than death."

He bleeds – the quivering arrow gnaws his breast;
He dies – and agonising sinks to rest.
Tradition tells the mournful tale,
And weeps at Sorrow's bloody wail;
Fell Superstition marks the place,
That sheltered Edmund's last distress;
And never, from that fateful day,
Have Hymen's votaries trod the way.
His spirit, by the pale moon light,
Flits there, each sad revolving night.

Anon. First published in The Suffolk Garland, 1819

Mark Taylor was born and raised in Bury St Edmunds. He was educated at Ipswich College of Art and The University of York, where he studied English Literature and Philosophy. He has been interested in Suffolk and East Anglian history, folklore and tradition for many years. Mark can be contacted via: hellofordaro@gmail.com

Visit secretsuffolk.com for a gazeteer of ancient and notable sites in Suffolk related to the story of Edmund, as well as news, reviews, photo galleries, interactive maps and more.

Visiting the magnificent city of York? Why not try our mobile app. Secret York peels back 2,000 years of history, revealing the hidden secrets of York's ancient past. For less than the price of a coffee you'll never need to buy a guidebook or guided tour again. Get the app for Android at bit.ly/17Xo1vh and Apple iOS at bit.ly/1fchumL

SECRET SUFFOLK
Discover Suffolk's ancient secrets

SECRET YORK
Discover York's ancient secrets